The Principles of
Entrepreneurial Progress

T0281878

Advance Praise for *The Principles of Entrepreneurial Progress*

"Fisher performs a remarkable act: distilling the essence of entrepreneurship into twelve core principles, spanning four critical areas: value, action, resources, and the big picture. Filled with pertinent and actionable insights, this book will ignite your entrepreneurial journey toward success."

—**Sophie Bacq**, Professor of Social Entrepreneurship, IMD

"Using an engaging and straightforward narrative, Fisher uses real-world stories to explain twelve principles—basic ideas and rules—that entrepreneurs can use to propel them throughout their entrepreneurial journey. By including explanations of each principle, suggestions for how to practice and apply them, and worksheets, this book provides practical and useful guidance, no matter where you are in your entrepreneurial career."

—**Melissa S. Cardon**, Haslam Distinguished Professor of Entrepreneurship & Innovation, Research Director, Anderson Center for Entrepreneurship & Innovation, Clark Family Faculty Research Fellow

"Dr. Greg Fisher has created a unique set of twelve core principles of entrepreneurial progress that cleverly lay out a roadmap for aspiring entrepreneurs to utilize. Written in an easily digestible form, this book offers a much-needed resource for anyone interested in establishing their own venture amidst the myriad of challenges they will confront."

—**Donald F. Kuratko**, The Jack M. Gill Distinguished Chair of Entrepreneurship & Professor of Entrepreneurship, Kelley School of Business, Indiana University-Bloomington

"Entrepreneurship is messy. What one starts out to create is rarely what gets created. The entrepreneur actually controls little and must continually learn and adapt as things unfold. In an excellent book, Fisher demonstrates that he gets entrepreneurship and provides a pathway for navigating this tumultuous journey. Using evidence-based principles and practical frameworks, he turns the unmanageable into the manageable."
—**Michael H. Morris**, Professor of Entrepreneurship & Social Innovation, University of Notre Dame

"Written from Fisher's unique and engaging perspective as a renowned researcher, professor, and former entrepreneur, *The Principles of Entrepreneurial Progress* is an invaluable resource for entrepreneurs, mentors, and educators. It offers practical insights and actionable strategies for driving entrepreneurial success and growth. Each principle is vividly illustrated, grounded in evidence, and shown to have crucial value for all types of entrepreneurs."
—**Chad Navis**, Arthur M. Spiro Professor of Entrepreneurial Leadership, Clemson University

"Whether entrepreneurs are working on effectively telling their story, prototyping their initial ideas, or facing some other quandary, Fisher offers a critically important text that explains various principles of how entrepreneurship works and offers frameworks for entrepreneurs to solve their problems systematically. Principles of Entrepreneurial Progress is the most 'entrepreneurship' text since *The Lean Startup!*"
—**Justin W. Webb**, Belk Distinguished Professor of Business Innovation, UNC Charlotte

The Principles
of Entrepreneurial
Progress

How to Create and Sustain Momentum
When Launching a Startup

GREG FISHER

OXFORD
UNIVERSITY PRESS

OXFORD
UNIVERSITY PRESS

Oxford University Press is a department of the University of Oxford. It furthers
the University's objective of excellence in research, scholarship, and education
by publishing worldwide. Oxford is a registered trade mark of Oxford University
Press in the UK and certain other countries.

Published in the United States of America by Oxford University Press
198 Madison Avenue, New York, NY 10016, United States of America.

CIP data is on file at the Library of Congress

ISBN 978-0-19-766982-2 (pbk.)
ISBN 978-0-19-766981-5 (hbk.)

DOI: 10.1093/oso/9780197669815.001.0001

Paperback printed by Marquis Book Printing, Canada
Hardback printed by Bridgeport National Bindery, Inc., United States of America

Contents

PART IV. THE BIG PICTURE PRINCIPLES

Acknowledgments: Haley Dosenbach and Ali N. Ferguson

This project benefited significantly from the input and contributions of Haley Dosenbach and Ali N. Ferguson. **Haley Dosenbach** researched many of the entrepreneurial stories shared in the book, and she wrote initial drafts of some of the stories to incorporate into the book. Additionally, she worked through most of the book chapters and provided an initial edit on each chapter. I am immensely grateful for her contributions to this book and the support and input she provided in the writing process. **Ali Ferguson** extensively edited a draft copy of the complete book. Her professionalism, encouragement, and attention to detail helped make the book manuscript better. I am grateful to her for how she helped push this book toward the finish line.

Introduction

It was late—much later than I usually fall asleep—yet I lay awake in the dark of my bedroom, staring at the ceiling, struggling to sleep. I was frustrated and perplexed. I was disappointed in myself that I did not have the answers.

Earlier that day, I had met with Richard, one of my former MBA students. Eight months prior, he had left his full-time job as a consultant with a well-known consulting firm to develop and launch the venture concept he had come up with in my entrepreneurship class a few years before. He had done well in the class. He was an active participant in the class case-study discussions, and he had taken the insights generated from those case discussions and applied them to the venture concept he was developing—a credit-scoring tool utilizing data from individuals' social media profiles and connections to assess their likelihood of repaying loans.

He had surmised that such a tool could be used as a complement to or substitute for traditional credit scores, such as those generated by Trans Union, Equifax, or Experian, which primarily use prior repayment information to generate a credit score. Richard envisaged that his tool might have valuable applications in emerging markets and lower-income communities where traditional repayment information and other credit-scoring data are typically scarce or nonexistent.

Richard seemed to be the right person to be working on this idea: he had expertise in web and data scraping, content analysis, machine learning, and artificial intelligence, and he had previously

The Principles of Entrepreneurial Progress. Greg Fisher, Oxford University Press.
© Oxford University Press 2024. DOI: 10.1093/oso/9780197669815.003.0001

worked on multiple consulting projects for clients in the financial services sector. As far as I could tell, he had done his research around the idea, articulated a significant gap in the market, and established a strong and compelling vision for his newly formed entity. He had also developed a detailed set of financial projections that reflected smooth and consistent revenue growth soon after launching the product. Plus, he expected to reach profitability approximately 16 months after first launching his product. His assumptions seemed sound, and the sophistication of his Excel spreadsheets was impressive, to say the least. He had even managed to raise a small amount of seed capital from two angel investors who had bought into his idea, and he had invested a significant amount of his personal savings to keep the venture afloat in the early phases of development.

From what I could tell, he had taken all the necessary steps to plan and implement his idea. Yet, he was clearly struggling to get traction. Although some clients appeared genuinely interested when he first approached them, almost all disappeared and were much more difficult to contact and pin down after a meeting or two. They just ghosted him.

Richard was confused and overwhelmed, and he had come to me looking for advice. I really wanted to help, but I didn't know what to say. I mumbled a few pithy lines of advice and offered some vague suggestions when I met him over coffee earlier that day, but I knew I had not given him anything concrete or meaningful. So, I lay in bed frustrated and perplexed.

"What's the right way to think about succeeding as an entrepreneur?" I wondered to myself as I lay awake that night. Can entrepreneurship be distilled down to a core set of ideas or principles that, if applied consistently, would help Richard and others like him navigate the complexity and uncertainty of embarking on the entrepreneurial journey?

As a researcher and teacher of entrepreneurship, I should have been able to answer this question, but for the longest time, I grappled for answers. No doubt, starting a new venture is *challenging*. There are lots of moving parts, many things that need to be taken care of, and an array of things that can go horribly wrong. In fact, as Richard's story illustrates, it can be downright overwhelming. That's part of the reason so many new ventures fail. When launching a new venture, entrepreneurs are pulled in many different directions by myriad different issues—legal concerns, financial challenges, marketing opportunities, people difficulties, operational bottlenecks, product problems, accounting puzzles, and so on and so on. It can all be too much!

Yet, despite these difficulties, there are people who succeed. We often celebrate these people and share their stories broadly. However, few people ever step back to consider whether there are valuable patterns, ideas, concepts, or perspectives that are applied consistently by those who succeed and are often overlooked by those who fail. What is it that allows some people to navigate the uncertainty, complexity, and ambiguity of launching a new venture while most people fail?

Since that time 15 years ago when I struggled to offer valuable answers and insights to Richard, I have woken up every day seeking to solve the entrepreneurship puzzle. As an entrepreneurship teacher and researcher, I have been obsessed with peeling back the layers of entrepreneurial stories to generate new theoretical and empirical insights into the entrepreneurial journey. I have endeavored to rigorously understand and unpack the actions that entrepreneurs take on a day-to-day basis to make productive progress in their endeavors. What do they do to manufacture momentum amid all the uncertainty?

Even with my obsession, making sense of what entrepreneurs do to succeed is not easy. The entrepreneurial journey is not simple or straightforward.

The Entrepreneurial Journey

The big picture of the entrepreneurial journey from idea to a viable growing entity is often depicted as a smooth upwardly sloping trajectory—like the one Richard put in his PowerPoint deck based on his financial projections and as depicted in Figure I.1. According to this depiction, an entrepreneur starts small, engages in a few repeatable and controllable activities, and thereby progresses systematically toward higher volumes of sales and revenues. Look at almost any PowerPoint deck for a new venture and you will see something that reflects this trajectory. I know. I have often been guilty of telling entrepreneurs they need to include it in their presentations.

However, my exposure to lots of entrepreneurs and their real, raw, unvarnished stories suggests that this couldn't be further from the truth. Entrepreneurial journeys are not smooth trajectories. They are not systematic, and they are definitely not predictable. They are messy. Really messy. The day-to-day activities of founders are usually chaotic. Many days, their paths appear to regress as they strive to move forward. It's frustrating, it's challenging, and it can

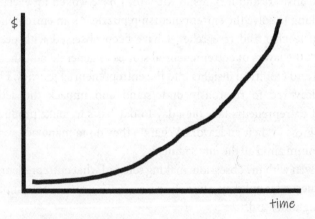

Figure I.1 The imagined startup path.

Figure I.2 The real startup path.

be downright defeating. The uncertainty, complexity, and ambiguity confronting an entrepreneur creates a tangled and erratic process of obstacles and challenges, as depicted in Figure I.2.

Generating Momentum through Microbursts of Progress

Nevertheless, those who succeed find a way to persist despite having to navigate such a mess. One way they do so is by focusing much less on the eventual outcome of an entrepreneurial endeavor and much more on simply making productive progress from one day to the next. They work toward just moving, generating momentum in their ventures through small bursts of day-to-day progress. They strive for what I call *microbursts of progress*—the day-to-day execution of immediate progressive steps that generate small wins and manufacture momentum for a venture amid all the chaos, as depicted in Figure I.3.

Despite their importance in moving ventures forward, knowing what to do to generate meaningful microbursts of progress can be

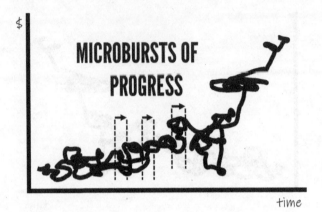

Figure I.3 The real startup path with microbursts of progress.

tricky. Because entrepreneurship is so complex, uncertain, and ambiguous, it is very difficult, if not impossible, to come up with a step-by-step recipe for success. Although some people have tried, success recipes in entrepreneurship typically have limited applicability across a broad range of scenarios. Trying to concoct a recipe for entrepreneurial success is a little like a chef—say, Gordon Ramsay, Rachael Ray, or Jamie Oliver—trying to devise a cooking recipe for a delicious dish when the ingredients, utensils, and timing differ each time the recipe is used. It's impossible. Likewise, it's impossible to devise a recipe for entrepreneurial success as the products, technologies, timing, people, and relationships change from one entrepreneurial journey to the next.

So, what do master chefs do to overcome this challenge? Instead of learning recipes, they learn *principles*.

Principles

The Cambridge Dictionary defines a principle as "a basic idea or rule that explains or controls how something happens or works."

A principle is more fundamental and more generally applicable than a method or approach. A method or approach is a specific way of doing something, usually following a set of steps or procedures to achieve a particular goal. In contrast, a principle is a fundamental truth or proposition that serves as the foundation for a system that generates an outcome. A method or approach may entail the practical application of a principle and may change depending on the situation, yet a principle remains constant and is applicable across various situations.

A principle is also distinct from a mechanism. A mechanism refers to the physical, mechanical, or social processes that are involved in the operation of a system or machine. It is the actual workings of something, the literal or figurative cogs that create an outcome. On the other hand, a principle refers to an underlying concept or theory that governs how something works. It is the fundamental idea or belief that guides the mechanism.

When preparing food, a cooking principle can be applied across a range of scenarios with different ingredients, utensils, and timing. For instance, the conduction principle in cooking stipulates that heat can move from one item to another via direct contact and that water is a better conductor of heat than air. Accordingly, as an example of how this principle can be applied, a turnip will cook faster in 212-degree boiling water than in a 400-degree oven. Instead of memorizing hundreds of recipes, top chefs learn the principles of cooking and then apply them in different situations to adapt to the ingredients, utensils, and timing at their disposal.

I was struck by the importance of principles when reading Greg McKeown's (2021: 156) book *Effortless*. In the book, he explained how principles can help us understand things at a fundamental level and generate knowledge that can be reapplied many times in many different scenarios. He said, "Principles are like the building blocks of knowledge: once you understand them correctly you can apply them hundreds of times." McKeown also quoted Harrington Emerson, the American engineer who made substantial contributions to the field of management. Emerson said, "As to methods, there may be a million and then some, but principles are few. The man who grasps principles can successfully select his own methods. The man who tries methods, ignoring principles is sure to have trouble" (McKeown, 2021: 156).

Elon Musk is reportedly also a big believer in taking the time to understand and apply basic scientific and organizational principles to establish a foundation to develop new business concepts and ideas. He said, "It's important to view knowledge as sort of a semantic tree—make sure you understand the *fundamental principles*, i.e., the trunk and the big branches, before you get into the leaves/details or there is nothing for them to hang on to," as reported on the *Farnam Street* blog (Farnam Street, 2021). James Clear reports that Musk attributes his success in building Tesla and SpaceX to what he refers to as "first principles thinking"—the practice of actively questioning every assumption about a given problem or scenario and then creating new solutions from scratch based on foundational ideas and concepts. Clear tells the story of Musk begging his long-term quest to send a rocket to Mars. He ran into a major challenge right off the bat. After visiting several aerospace manufacturers across the globe, Musk discovered that the cost of purchasing a rocket was astronomical—up to $65 million. Given the high price, he began to rethink the problem. "I tend to approach things from a physics framework," Musk said in an interview. "Physics teaches you to reason from first principles rather than by analogy. So, I said, okay, let's look at the first principles. What is a rocket made of? Aerospace-grade aluminum alloys, plus some titanium, copper, and carbon fiber. Then I asked, what is the value of those materials on the commodity market? It turned out that the materials cost of a rocket was around two percent of the typical price." (Clear, n.d.). Instead of buying a finished rocket for tens of millions, Musk decided to create his own company, purchase the raw materials for cheap, and build the rockets himself. SpaceX was born. Within a few years, SpaceX had cut the price of launching a rocket by nearly 10 times while still making a profit. Musk used first principles thinking to break the situation down to the fundamentals, bypass the high prices of the aerospace industry, and create a more effective solution.

When I first read this discussion about principles and thought through these various quotes about the importance of principles, I was both excited and perplexed. I was excited because the concept seemed so valuable, so foundational, and so applicable, but I was perplexed because I had no idea what I might identify as the principles of the core knowledge for the topic I care most about: entrepreneurship.

Principles in Entrepreneurship

Are there foundational concepts and ideas that generate meaningful progress and momentum in an entrepreneurial endeavor? Can entrepreneurship be distilled down to a core set of basic principles? Are there ways that entrepreneurs can think and act across a range of different scenarios that will generate the microbursts of progress they need to move their ideas forward from one day to the next?

These are the questions I tackle in this book.

Although much has been written about entrepreneurship and the process of starting a new venture, my goal is to distill entrepreneurship down to a core set of principles. Acting according to these principles can make a big difference to those who want to launch a new venture or are currently in the process of doing so. Many of these principles underlie popular methods or approaches for launching an entrepreneurial endeavor, such as the lean startup approach (Ries, 2011) or the effectual method to venture creation (Sarasvathy, 2009). Yet breaking down such principles and disentangling them from the more complex method or approach of which they are part makes them more understandable and more actionable.

As with a principle-based perspective in cooking, or in science, or in life more generally, some principles are more relevant, appropriate, and impactful in certain situations and other principles are more relevant, appropriate, and impactful in other situations. The role of the person applying such principles is to discern when a principle should be emphasized. For example, when a chef uses cooking principles to create a meal, as discussed earlier, they don't need to use all the principles of food preparation in all instances of preparing a dish. Rather, the role of the chef is to discern which principles are relevant and apply the relevant principles in the appropriate scenario. The same concept applies to an entrepreneur. The principles of entrepreneurial progress don't all need to be applied all the time; the role of the entrepreneur is to discern which principles are relevant for making progress in the scenario they confront as they develop their new venture. Properly understanding each of the principles will empower an entrepreneur to discern when each should be applied.

The principles of entrepreneurial progress are what I wish I had at my disposal when I lay awake that night wondering how I could help Richard. They encompass the basic knowledge and perspectives I wish I had when I embarked on my own entrepreneurial journey many years ago prior to entering academia. They reflect the best of what I have seen in the hundreds of entrepreneurial case studies I have read, in the thousands of entrepreneurial podcasts I have listened to, and in the dozens of different startups I have worked with over the years. They encompass some of the concepts that readers of *Entrepreneur Magazine* found to be very useful within the many articles I wrote for that outlet over the years.

The principles distilled here also highlight some of the most interesting and insightful findings from recent academic research on entrepreneurship—these include findings from my own research and the research of many of my smart and perceptive colleagues studying entrepreneurship in business schools across the globe. In recent years, many of the most interesting and relevant academic research findings from organizational psychology and associated disciplines have been packaged into impactful books and delivered to broader audiences by authors like Adam Grant, Amy Edmondson, and Scott Sonenshein. However, many of the most interesting and relevant academic research findings from entrepreneurship studies have remained hidden from broader audiences behind the veil of academia, locked away in academic journals and sealed off by institutional paywalls.

In sharing the principles distilled in this book, I pull back that veil and highlight what one can learn and apply from some of the recent academic studies on entrepreneurship and related phenomena.

This book is for those who are on the precipice of starting something new. It is for those young professionals and business school students who have a gutsy determination to create and grow a new enterprise and for those who are older, more seasoned, and want to reinvigorate their careers by launching a new business that leverages some of their experience and expertise. That said, entrepreneurs work under conditions of uncertainty as competitors are constantly acting themselves, technology changes, political and legal shifts happen, and the economy evolves through cycles. Therefore, even though these principles increase an entrepreneur's chance of making meaningful progress, they don't guarantee success. You can and should apply these principles to enhance your potential for success, but it's not guaranteed. Success is never a sure thing.

This book is also for business school professors and others who teach entrepreneurship. It can be used in class to provide practical evidence-based insights about what it takes to get started and sustain momentum in a new venture, and the 12 principles discussed fit very nicely into a 12- to 16-week semester as each week can be dedicated to a single principle.

Finally, the book can serve as a lifeline, inspiration, and guide to those who are already in the entrepreneurial arena, those who are in the midst of starting a new venture and want to generate and sustain momentum in what they are doing. This book is for all the people who find themselves in Richard's position—they have been brave enough to take the leap but have stalled and now need to reinvigorate their entrepreneurial journeys. It will help them check whether they are thinking and acting in ways that will generate microbursts of progress and provide guidance as to additional things they can do to keep moving forward on their entrepreneurial journeys. These are ideas that make a real difference in the life of an entrepreneur and in the journey of a startup venture.

The Buckets

The principles shared in this book can be divided into four buckets: the value bucket, the action bucket, the resource bucket, and the big picture bucket, as depicted in Figure I.4.

The *value bucket* encompasses six principles that empower entrepreneurs to create something of value, not just valuable to them but valuable to a broad base of users. This is the primary goal of any entrepreneur. It sounds simple, but achieving this goal is often very hard. At the start of their entrepreneurial journeys, most founders think they have a clear idea of what they are going to do to create value for prospective customers, yet many times they learn that users don't care about what they initially conceived. Value creation is more of a discovery process than an initial conception or grand idea, and the principles in the value bucket will help founders and their teams discover what customers and others perceive to be valuable so they can provide true value via their products or services. The principles in the value bucket are discussed in Part I of the book.

The *action bucket* encompasses two principles about how founders should act to make progress in their entrepreneurial journeys. These principles are drawn from studying what entrepreneurs actually do, examining how they act from one day to

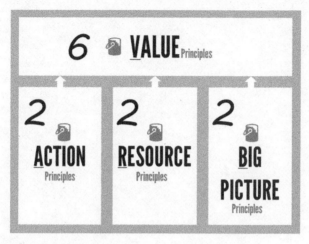

Figure I.4 The four buckets capturing the principles of entrepreneurial progress.

the next. The principles in the action bucket are discussed in Part II of the book.

The *resource bucket* encompasses two principles pertaining to resourcing a new venture. Entrepreneurs are almost always resource constrained—they typically don't have all the resources they need to do what they want to do. However, to make progress, they need to overcome and go beyond these constraints. The principles in the resource bucket empower founders to do this. The principles in the resource bucket are discussed in Part III of the book.

The *big picture bucket* encompasses two principles related to the holistic aspects of the entrepreneurial journey. These principles help entrepreneurs appreciate and understand the integrated nature of entrepreneurship and empower founders to think and act in accordance with this more integrated perspective. The principles in the big picture bucket are discussed in Part IV of the book.

PART I
THE VALUE PRINCIPLES

1

The Problem Principle

Living in San Francisco is expensive—very expensive—especially for people with no large exit payouts or big salaries from working in the booming tech sector in that region. This was a serious issue for two young East Coast imports, early in their careers, trying to make it as designers in the Bay Area. Joe Gebbia (2017) explained on the *How I Built This* podcast how he and Brian Chesky had become best friends while attending the Rhode Island School of Design (RISD) and how, after graduation, Brian had moved to Los Angeles to launch his career as an industrial designer, while Joe moved to San Francisco to work as an entry-level designer for Chronicle Books.

While at RISD, the two often had discussions about starting a business, but Joe had taken things a step further by creating a new product he called CritBuns, a uniquely designed portable foam seat cushion. "Frustrated by the lack of design on the market for a simple seat cushion, Joe brought his own perspective to create a new one altogether. He started with the problem: long, uncomfortable art critiques spent sitting on hard surfaces, and answered with a solution: a uniquely designed, portable foam seat cushion" is how the original CritBuns website described the story behind the product (Critbuns, n.d.). The business was not an immediate raging success, but Joe did manage to sell 800 buns to RISD as a graduation present for his graduating class. He also got orders for his unique product from people inside and beyond his network. He continued to work on CritBuns as a side hustle after starting his design job at Chronicle Books.

A few months after Joe and Brian trekked out west, Brian was miserable in his job in LA, and a room opened up in Joe's loft in San Francisco. Brian resigned and moved in with Joe, uncertain what he was going to do next. Soon after that, their landlord jacked up the rent, and the two of them panicked. The previous rent had already stretched them; now, it was untenable. But it was a cool loft.

In his TED Talk many years later (Gebbia, 2016), Joe described how a few days after receiving the letter from their landlord, he sent the following email to Brian.

From: joe
Date: September 22, 2007
To: Brian
Subject: subletter

brian
i thought of a way to make a few bucks—turning our place into "designers bed and breakfast"—offering young designers who come into town a place crash during the 4 day event, complete with wireless Internet, a small desk space, sleeping mat, and breakfast each morning. Ha!

joe

Joe further explained in his TED Talk that from there, "We built a basic website, and Air Bed and Breakfast was born. Three lucky guests (Kat, Amol, and Michael) got to stay on a $20 airbed on the hardwood floor, but they loved it, and so did we. I swear, the ham and Swiss cheese omelets we made tasted totally different because we made them for our guests. We took them on adventures around the city, and when we said goodbye to the last guest, the door latch clicked, and Brian and I just stared at each other. Did we just discover it was possible to make friends while also making rent? The wheels had started to turn. My old roommate Nate Blecharczyk joined as engineering cofounder. And we buckled down to see if we could turn this into a business" (Gebbia, 2016).

Now, it was not a quick and easy path from there to the Airbnb we know today. It was messy; difficult; frustrating; and, at times, very disappointing. However, one of the things that kept Joe, Brian, and Nathan going through the ups and downs—the false starts, credit card debt, and investor rejection—was that they understood and believed in the *problem* they were solving. They had experienced that problem themselves and seen firsthand how their solution could address a real need.

At the core of the founding of Airbnb was a problem that the founders sought to solve. The problem is what got them going.

A decade before Joe and Brian were hosting their first guests in their San Francisco "air bed and breakfast," Sara Blakely was trying to fix a very different problem—panty lines. On the *How I Built This* podcast, Sara described how, as a young door-to-door fax machine salesperson working for Danka, she liked to make a good impression when dropping in on clients, and that included dressing well. However, after purchasing a relatively expensive pair of white slacks, she couldn't find any underwear that didn't show through. In desperation, she cut the feet off a pair of pantyhose and wore them as underwear. It worked! The white slacks looked great, and she felt comfortable and confident (Blakely, 2017).

She started to think that within her desperate solution to an intimate personal dilemma, a product may exist. She spent the next two years and $5,000 in personal savings researching and developing her hosiery idea of "feetless pantyhose" while still selling fax machines. When she eventually launched her product, she called it Spanx! She had to hustle to get the product into stores and to capture the attention of key influencers, but a few months later, Oprah Winfrey named Spanx one of her "Favorite Things," which led to a significant rise in popularity and sales, as well as Sara's resignation from Danka. In 2012, Sara landed on the cover of *Forbes* magazine for being the youngest self-made female billionaire in the world.

Sara Blakely landed on the cover of *Forbes* because she set out to solve a real problem.

Around the time Sara's new product was being featured on Oprah's "Favorite Things," Perry Chen, a musician living in New Orleans, was experiencing a very different challenge. Perry had grown up on Roosevelt Island in New York City with his mother, a social worker, and his father, a schoolteacher. When it came time for college, he moved to New Orleans to attend Tulane. While there, he became increasingly involved in the local music scene, and after graduating, he stayed in New Orleans and continued to pursue a musical path. When preparing for the 2001 JazzFest, Chen wrote to the Austrian DJ duo Kruder & Dorfmeister, asking what it would cost to bring them to New Orleans for a show during JazzFest. They wanted $15,000 and five business-class tickets—not an insurmountable sum but one that Chen had no hope of pulling together himself.

"I had this feeling that this was a problem that should be solvable," he said. "There was a possibility that the artists would have a great show, and everybody would have a great time. But none of that could happen because the decision had to be made by me—based on my own resources. There was an inherent flaw in that" (Chafkin, 2013).

The fact that Perry had not been able to pull off bringing Kruder & Dorfmeister to JazzFest bugged him, and he realized it was emblematic of a bigger issue in funding creative pursuits. He stewed on the issue for many years, and during that time, he pondered potential solutions for funding such creative projects. A few years later, Perry was back living in New York City and waiting tables to afford to live. One of the regulars in the Brooklyn restaurant where he worked was music journalist Yancey Strickler; the two became friends. Perry shared his desire to create a way to fund creative pursuits, and the pair decided to do something about it. They later added a third member to the team, Charles Adler, and between the three of them, they designed a website that would be launched in 2009 as Kickstarter—an online platform where creative people could share their ideas with a broad audience who could pledge money to support an idea. Under the "Kickstarter FAQ—The Basics" (Kickstarter, n.d.) section of the original Kickstarter website, they said this:

"We believe that ...

- A good idea, communicated well, can spread fast and wide.
- A large group of people can be a tremendous source of money and encouragement."

The website went on to point out:

People who use Kickstarter to fund their projects ("project creators") keep 100% ownership and control. Project creators can offer products, services or other benefits ("rewards") to inspire people to support their project: A hot-air balloon ride to the first person to pledge $300, an invitation to the BBQ for anyone who pledges more than $5, exclusive daily video updates for anyone who pledges more than $1. It's up to each project creator to sculpt their own offers and there's lots of cool ways to do it. People who pledge also receive access to all project updates (posts, video, pics, etc.). "Project Updates" is our fancy name for the project blog. Some project creators may post 10 updates a day, others may rarely post. Some may make all their posts publicly viewable, others may set all their posts as exclusive to their backers (Kickstarter, n.d.).

As of September 2021, the "Stats" section of the Kickstarter website reported that the venture has received more than $6 billion in pledges from more than 20 million backers to fund more than 208,000 projects, such as films, music, stage shows, comics, journalism, video games, technology, publishing, and food-related projects.

The Principle

What do all three of these founding stories have in common?

One thing that they have in common is that in each case, the founders were certainly not obviously qualified to be pursuing the opportunity at hand. They didn't have relevant industry experience, a specialized education or skillset, significant resources, or even much entrepreneurship experience. In fact, on the surface, they had no business doing what they were doing, but they did it anyway.

However, what they did have was a *problem* that they sought to solve. Joe and Brian were solving their "rent" problem, Sara was solving her "panty line" problem, and Perry was solving his "creative project financing" problem.

In each case, a clear problem not only fueled the founders to start a venture but also kept them focused and motivated as they ran into difficulties in developing their ideas. A problem provides focus. It generates a reason for being and a reason to keep going. It provides energy and impetus. Having a clear, identifiable problem to solve can make up for many other deficiencies in a startup team.

In the book *Super Founders*, venture capitalist and author Ali Tamaseb (2021) reported on his data-driven analysis of unicorn ventures—startup ventures that had scaled into private firms with a valuation exceeding a billion dollars. He sought to answer the question, "What did billion-dollar startups look like when they were getting started?" He also gathered the same data on nonunicorn startups so he could accurately compare what differentiates billion-dollar startups from those that failed to reach that significant benchmark. All in all, he ended up with more than 30,000 data points in his analysis.

So what did all this data tell us?

Well, quite a bit. But one of the core conclusions that Tamaseb (2021: 259) drew was this: "What matters is that as the founder, you have thought deeply about your startup—you can pinpoint exactly what problem you're solving and for whom. If you have to list five bullet points for the problems you are solving, and five bullet points for your value proposition, and bullet points for why now is the best time, think harder, get to the root. Try to understand the one thing that you really are solving, who is really the customer, the one key value proposition, the one reason that makes today the ideal time to start this business."

In contrast to examining how successful founders tend to focus on a clear and identifiable problem as an impetus to develop their ventures, one can also consider what *mistakes* unsuccessful founders make. Why do startups fail? CB Insights (2021), a market intelligence and data analysis firm that tracks startup ventures, reported on their analysis of 111 postmortems of failed startups since 2018. From this analysis, they learned that "there is rarely one reason for a single startup's failure." However, they did "begin to see a pattern to these [failure] stories." The second most cited reason for failure was "no market need." In other words, the failed ventures were addressing issues that were "interesting to solve rather than those that serve a market need" (the most highly cited reason for failure was that a venture "ran out of cash/failed to raise new capital," which usually happens because a venture is not addressing a valid market need).

A salient and high-profile example of venture failure due to "no market need" comes from the mobile-focused streaming service Quibi, which shut down in October 2020, just six months after launching and raising a mammoth $1.8 billion. Quibi was set up to be a short-form streaming platform that would generate content for viewing on mobile devices. The service aimed to target a younger demographic with TV-style content delivered in 10-minute episodes called "quick bites" (which the name Quibi was derived from: "QUI-ck BI-tes"). The service was founded by Jeffrey Katzenberg. Meg Whitman joined as CEO.

However, Quibi did not really solve a user need, and after shutting down, Katzenberg and Whitman wrote a letter to employees stating that the idea behind Quibi "wasn't strong enough to justify a stand-alone streaming service" (as reported by Mullin, Flint, and Farrell [2020] in the *Wall Street Journal*). At its core, Quibi was not solving a significant problem for its users. Thus, despite obscene amounts of funding and some of the best talent in the business, the venture failed to get significant traction. They overlooked the first principle of entrepreneurial progress:

The Problem Principle:
Entrepreneurial progress entails identifying *a meaningful problem to solve.*

A meaningful problem is a problem that

- you care about and are willing to dedicate a lot of time and energy to resolve it;
- a significant number of other people find frustrating and would be delighted to have a solution handy to address the problem; and
- a problem that you think is addressable, meaning that with an investment of time and energy, a solution is likely to be developed.

Identifying a meaningful problem to solve not only empowers founders to make progress in getting started but also sustains founding teams as they hit roadblocks and run into difficulties along their entrepreneurial journeys. It is an antidote to arriving at a place where there is "no market need."

The Practice

Although Joe, Brian (Airbnb), Sara (Spanx), and Perry (Kickstarter) uncovered problems due to personal challenges and difficulties, not all ventures are born out of problems experienced directly by founders. Some founders are more strategic and deliberate in analyzing an external problem they seek to solve.

I recall the MBA class in which Stacy Brewer announced that she wanted to help address the education crisis in South Africa. Stacy had not experienced the problem herself as she had gone to a reputable private high school in Johannesburg and graduated from a renowned South African university, and here she was, sitting in an MBA class at the Gordon Institute of Business Science (GIBS), the best business school in Africa. However, she had analyzed the data. She told the class that "South Africa ranked 140th out of 144 countries on the quality of the education system in the World Economic Forum's 'Global Competitiveness Report,' the quality of primary school education ranked 133rd, the quality of math and science education ranked 144th, and Internet access at schools ranked 117th."

She surmised that South Africa's prospects as a country were poor unless the education issues were addressed. Off the back of this, she explained her vision for a network of highly affordable, low-cost private schools that would leverage technology to deliver an excellent educational experience to South African kids. Although some of her classmates thought she was biting off more than she could chew or perhaps being a little too idealistic, she ignored their smirks and pressed on. One of the reasons she could do this was that she had taken the time to analyze and understand the problem she sought to solve. It was large. It was important. But even if she only partially addressed it, she would make a huge difference and be successful.

In 2012, soon after completing her MBA, Stacy cofounded SPARK Schools with her classmate Ryan Harrison. One of the reasons she was able to raise the capital needed to support her idea—from both local and global investors—was that she was seeking to solve a big problem that many people cared about. Since then, the SPARK Schools network has expanded to serve 13,500

SPARK scholars at 17 campuses in South Africa, as per the SPARK Schools website.

So how does one analyze a problem to facilitate progress and generate momentum in the entrepreneurial journey?

Well, one valuable way to do so is to adopt the perspective of a journalist. Journalists are trained to use the Five Ws approach to understand and describe an issue when researching and writing a story. This entails asking "who," "what," "when," "where," and "why" about the issue at hand. "Referring back to the Five 'W's helps journalists address the fundamental questions that every story should be able to answer," according to a Luke Burns (2017) article in the *New Yorker*. Just as journalists seek to garner a deeper and more complete understanding of the issues they are writing about, founders can seek to generate a deeper and more complete understanding of the problem they seek to solve by asking the following:

- What problem are we addressing?
- Who has this problem?
- When do users have the problem?
- Where do users have the problem?
- Why do users have the problem?

And, just as journalists sometimes add a sixth element to their Five Ws framework by asking "how," founders can add a sixth element to their Five Ws:

- How are users currently solving or working around the problem?

Asking these questions helps generate a deeper perspective and understanding of the problem to be solved that can be used down the line to more adequately develop truly useful and appealing solutions. Without being stretched by the Five Ws, the inclination of most founders who are early in their entrepreneurial journeys is to describe the focal problem quite simplistically, usually by merely specifying what problem they are addressing.

However, going beyond the what to the who, when, where, why, and how can help founders and founding teams start to see a problem in a new light (when and where), get much more in tune with their target customers (who), understand the root cause of the problem (why), and begin to assess the substitute products that they may ultimately be competing with (how).

Especially important here is for an entrepreneur to research, evaluate, and broadly consider *how the problem is currently solved.* This includes understanding what workarounds users might be using to solve the problem and carefully and diligently assessing the competitors that may already be out there. Understanding the competitive landscape and assessing each competitor's key product offering, strategy, resources, capabilities, and key assumptions can provide an entrepreneur with a clear, real, and important perspective of the competitive domain in which they will operate. Doing this also lays the foundation for focusing on opportunities for differentiation and additional value creation in that competitive domain.

The level of depth you generate in answering these questions depends on how serious you are about the venture you wish to build and how much you want to ensure that you are developing your venture on a solid foundation. If you provide just short, few-word answers to each of these questions without thinking about or researching them much, then you are likely to not have much of a foundation for the rest of the entrepreneurial journey. But the opposite is also an issue. It is possible to get so trapped in answering each of these questions and researching your responses that you never move beyond this to take the needed entrepreneurial action. Therefore, it is important to dedicate enough time, energy, and perspective to generate solid, well-grounded research to each question but to not become overly obsessed with answering each such question that you are never able to move on.

The Tool

So, how can you organize your thinking or facilitate a meaningful discussion around the problem that you seek to address in your startup? Well, one way is to use the Five Ws worksheet, which specifies the critical questions in relation to the problem you seek to address and provides space for you to capture your answers, as depicted in Figure 1.1.

If you are a solo founder, you can carry out this exercise individually. However, even in that case, avoid the temptation to just see this as another task to be completed; don't superficially fill out the worksheet and be done with it. Instead, really engage with the questions. Carefully consider the answers. As Steve Blank, the renowned startup educator and author, likes to say, "There are no facts inside your building, so get outside. . . . Facts live outside the building, where future customers live and work" (Blank and Dorf, 2020). This advice is highly applicable to doing research on

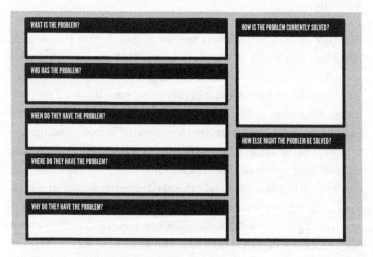

Figure 1.1 The Five Ws worksheet.

the what, who, when, where, why, and how of the problem you are solving. To do this, a founding can

- talk to the people experiencing the problem,
- observe them as they engage with the problem,
- interrogate the root cause of the problem, and
- evaluate what people are currently doing to get around the problem.

Here, it is valuable to assume the perspective of an anthropologist, attempting to get close to the subjects, to really understand what's going on, to peel back the nuance of their day-to-day practices, and to uncover hidden insights that may not be immediately obvious.

If you are working in a founding team, then work through this worksheet diligently as a team. Discuss, debate, and really interrogate your answers with your cofounders. Go out and do the anthropological work described above and come back and share your insights and perspectives with one another. Doing this as a team and agreeing on all aspects of the problem you seek to solve is one way to ensure you are aligned as you embark on the wild startup ride.

In some cases, a founder will stumble onto a big problem to be solved and will just keep working on that problem without ever really reflecting on it or thinking about it more deeply. However, this is the exception. In most cases, founders benefit immensely from spending a bit of time thinking deeply about the problem they seek to solve. The questions in the Five Ws worksheet can help you do this. By doing so, founders can more fully understand what they are doing, why they are doing it, who their target user is, and where they can help. This allows them to make meaningful microbursts of progress that accumulate to generate real momentum in a venture. This is what you want!

In the examples highlighted earlier in this chapter, founders Sara Blakely (Spanx), Perry Chen (Kickstarter), and Joe Gebbia and

Brian Chesky (Airbnb) may not have explicitly gone through the worksheet as laid out here, but they implicitly took time to understand the what, who, when, where, why, and how of the problem they were attempting to solve, and doing so laid a solid foundation for the venture they went on to deliver. It is possible to appreciate and understand the problem you are trying to solve without using the Five Ws worksheet, but using the worksheet provides structure and perspective to ensure that you are adequately focusing on an important problem as your core for developing a new venture.

Fully Embracing the Problem Principle on Your Entrepreneurial Journey

So, how do you know if you are fully embracing the problem principle as a means to make meaningful progress in your entrepreneurial endeavor? One way to assess this is to contrast what it looks like to fully and deeply embrace the problem principle versus what it looks like to overlook it or only superficially embrace it.

Fully embracing the problem principle on the entrepreneurial journey entails the following:

- Thinking deeply about the problem that you seek to solve
- Researching the problem you seek to solve from many different angles and perspectives
- Getting out of the building to interact with or observe users experiencing the problem
- Articulating multiple aspects or dimensions of the problem: what, who, when, where, why, and how
- Revisiting and updating the problem to be addressed again and again on your entrepreneurial journey
- Thinking about and discussing the problem to be solved with your founding team or other stakeholders

Ignoring or overlooking the problem principle on the entrepreneurial journey entails the following:

- Superficially thinking about and researching the problem that you seek to solve
- Never interacting with or observing users who experience the problem
- Articulating only one aspect or dimension of the problem
- Thinking about the problem that you seek to solve once and never revisiting it again on your entrepreneurial journey
- Thinking about the problem to be solved in isolation and never discussing it with your founding team or other stakeholders

Identifying, assessing, and understanding a key problem to solve is a critical element to any entrepreneurial journey. Doing so creates progress, and any founder who does this is going to establish a stronger foundation for their venture. But just identifying, assessing, and understanding a problem is not enough. You, as a startup founder, need to figure out what to do about that problem and then take action to bring that into reality. That's where the other principles of entrepreneurial progress come in. I turn to those next.

2

The Exploration Principle

The exploration principle specifies that to make progress in an entrepreneurial venture, one needs to deeply explore the domain in which that venture will operate and generate a large number of possible alternate solutions or concepts for solving the focal problem in that domain. On the one hand, this may seem like a fairly obvious principle for generating entrepreneurial progress; on the other hand, there are subtle insights underlying this principle that can be quite counterintuitive yet incredibly valuable. It is a principle that I have used many times to break out of a deadlock or a rut when writing this book. But more on that later.

To understand the essence of the principle, let's examine the story of Jen Rubio, the cofounder of Away, the hot direct-to-consumer travel brand. Jen emigrated from the Philippines to New Jersey with her family when she was 7, and as one might guess, growing up as a first-generation immigrant wasn't easy. In New Jersey, she was the girl with an accent who ate different food. She was also put into lower-level classes because she was an English-as-a-second-language student. She gritted out her K–12 education and ended up going to college at Penn State University. However, Jen found college boring and left when she was 20.

After school, Jen juggled jobs and eventually became a social media consultant—before that title even existed. Initially, she managed social media for a local cafe, but over time, she grew her client base to include a variety of different businesses. This background led her to become head of social media at Warby Parker in 2011. Her role at Warby Parker put her on the map for recruiters, and she was headhunted to take on an innovation role at All Saints based

The Principles of Entrepreneurial Progress. Greg Fisher, Oxford University Press.
© Oxford University Press 2024. DOI: 10.1093/oso/9780197669815.003.0003

in London. She loved to travel, and the extravagance of being in London appealed to her. She traveled a lot in that phase of her life—both for work and for pleasure.

On one of these trips, her suitcase broke in Zurich Airport, which embarrassingly resulted in her underwear being strewn across the airport floor. Jen reached out to her online social network to ask what new suitcase she should buy, but no one had a good answer. Furthermore, the process of trying to find and purchase a new suitcase from a retail store was horrible. It entailed overstocked, disorganized shop floors; pushy salespeople; and very little clear differentiation from one brand to the next. Jen shared her frustrations with fellow Warby Parker alum and friend Steph Korey. Steph was doing an MBA at Columbia at the time. The two of them recognized that luggage was a category that was ripe for disruption, so they decided to create a new luggage brand.

What did they do next?

Well, in Jen's words, they went "shopping, like, every single day. We went to every department store; we went to every luggage store and compared all the experiences and all the prices and kept very meticulous notes on what was out there" (Rubio, 2019). From their exploratory shopping efforts, they got a strong and definitive sense of what luggage options were available. However, they did not have a sense of what people really wanted in the perfect suitcase, so "over the course of a few months we talked to like maybe 800 people," said Jen, "and we would just talk to them about travel, and we would ask them . . . about their biggest pain points when they travel." This armed them with certain "stories that kept coming up," and that's how they figured out all of the things they "needed to make like our one perfect suitcase," reported Jen (Rubio, 2019). With this information, they were able to generate many possible rough designs to figure out which really hit the sweet spot.

Even though they faced a multitude of different challenges as they brought their product to market, including manufacturing difficulties, shipping delays, and airlines prohibiting suitcases with built-in cell phone chargers (a feature of their first suitcase), they still managed to create a beautiful, highly functional suitcase. This first suitcase was the foundation for what became a portfolio of val uable, sleek, and highly desirable travel products they trademarked under the brand name Away. In 2019, the company was valued at $1.4 billion after they raised $100 million to keep growing the Away brand.

The Principle

At their core, entrepreneurs are creative problem solvers. But how do successful entrepreneurs come up with creative ideas to solve problems? The answer: they explore and generate *lots* of possibilities.

One sure way to be creative is to explore and generate lots and lots of ideas. Most people think creativity is having lots of ideas, but anyone can generate lots of ideas if they are prompted or forced to. The really creative ideas—the ones that are both novel and useful— come from generating lots of ideas and then using those many ideas to identify what is most novel and valuable. When attempting to solve a problem, most people's natural tendency is to generate just a few ideas as possible solutions and then attempt to refine and im- prove one of those initial ideas. It's easy to get locked in on the first idea that you have for solving a problem. However, whether you are attempting to solve luggage challenges, panty lines, or creative project funding dilemmas, one way to give yourself the best chance of coming up with a really creative, innovative, and impactful solu- tion is to explore lots of possible solutions.

Adam Grant, the well-known organizational psychologist and author of the book *Originals*, reported that the data on highly cre- ative people shows that for the most part, their secret to creativity was not genius but rather generating lots of ideas. He said:

The great originals throughout history did not have few ideas, they had tons of them, and way more than most of their peers. If you look at musicians, for example—Mozart, Bach, Beethoven— their average hit rate is not any higher than many composers you have never heard of. What differentiates them is that they came up with a lot more ideas. . . . The reason for that is you have to generate a lot of variety to be original. If you just come up with a few ideas, your first few are usually the most obvious. You have to rule out the familiar in order to get to the novel. But most people never do that. They fall in love with their first idea, or they end up questioning whether they have the ability to come up with more ideas (Grant, 2016).

Since learning this insight and examining the empirical data supporting the notion that the best way to creatively solve problems is to explore and generate many possible solutions, I have used this idea multiple times to effectively get myself out of a jam—big or small.

In structuring and writing this book, I often came to a point where I didn't know what would come next. I didn't know the best way to convey a key idea or how to transition from one idea to the next or what words to use to make a story pop. Writing a book is a series of obstacles that need to be overcome, problems that need to be solved. By far the best strategy for navigating past each of these obstacles was to explore and generate lots of different possible solutions.

I would come to a point where I did not know what to write next. I would sit back in my chair and think about it, maybe even refer to a book from one of my favorite authors to get inspiration for how to move on, and I would invariably come up with one or two mostly obvious ideas. It was only when I forced myself to generate and explore 6, 8, or 12 different ideas that I was able to develop the less obvious, more creative ideas for moving on.

It initially takes work, effort, and mental energy to conceptualize and explore a greater number of ideas and solutions to key problems, but it is out of that work, effort, and mental energy that the most creative ideas are born. Additionally, the more you seek to explore multiple alternatives to solving a single problem, the easier it becomes to do so the next time. In other words, in the same way you get stronger the more you lift weights, the greater your capacity to generate divergent thoughts as you practice the skill. It is from these divergent thoughts that true innovation and creativity are born.

The Exploration Principle:
Entrepreneurial progress entails exploring your problem domain deeply and generating a *wide range of solutions* to solve the focal problem.

The exploration principle operates across two domains of exploration: problems and solutions. Regarding problems, the exploration principle entails fully exploring the problem to be tackled and addressed by an entrepreneurial endeavor. Using the Five Ws worksheet introduced in the prior chapter can help facilitate deeper exploration of the problem to be addressed. Regarding solutions, the exploration principle entails exploring many different possible solutions for addressing a problem, and this is the type of exploration I primarily address in the remainder of this chapter.

The Practice

Designers figured out this principle many years back. At the core of almost any design process is the notion of exploring lots of possible designs.

My first exposure to design thinking and the design process more generally was a 1999 *Nightline* documentary about the highly influential and upcoming (at the time) industrial design firm called IDEO. IDEO is now a recognized name in the business world, but in the late 1990s, at the time of the *Nightline* documentary (Nightline, 1999), the company was largely unknown outside of Silicon Valley. *Nightline's* feature became known as the "shopping cart documentary" and was largely credited with putting IDEO on the map. By 1999, IDEO had designed the first computer mouse for Apple, Nike sunglasses, and General Electric medical devices, along with many other products that we now take for granted.

Host Ted Koppel introduced the documentary by saying, "How does the process of designing a better product work? And would it be interesting to watch that process? ... Here was the premise of the program. We went to IDEO, the product design folk, and said take something old and familiar, like, say, the shopping cart, and completely redesign it for us in just five days."

In the documentary, the IDEO team was challenged to design a new shopping cart in five days. ABC's cameras followed the IDEO team around for all five days to get a clear conception of their design process. When I first watched this documentary, I was mesmerized for many reasons, but one thing that really struck me was that they basically spent four out of the five days exploring. It started with the team exploring the problem to be addressed from many different angles for the first day or two—they went out and observed people using shopping carts in grocery stores, talked to shop owners, photographed different types of customers, and classified customers into categories. The exploration then shifted to the generation of dozens of possible solutions. They captured all of these different ideas on paper sketches that were pasted on the wall for all to see.

The cultural norms of IDEO are all strongly oriented toward exploration. In the documentary, some of these norms, or mantras, were plastered on the walls to remind people to "encourage wild ideas," to "defer judgment," that "no idea is a bad idea," and to "build on the ideas of others."

On about the third day of the five-day process, the exploration shifted from drawing to building new ideas. The team homed in on four key concepts and started rapidly prototyping these concepts, building mockups of new shopping carts with whatever materials they could find. On the fourth day, they presented their mockups to one another, and only after that did they decide on a final version of the cart and start developing the end product. Essentially, to be good at generating valuable new ideas for clients, the IDEO team must be masters of exploration. They generate and explore many, many ideas to come up with the best ideas. From what I could tell, they spent 70% to 80% of their time exploring, to give themselves the best chance of generating a creative, innovative solution.

Since the "shopping cart documentary" in 1999, design thinking has become a cottage industry. There are books and magazine articles about design things, and an array of facilitators will take you through a design thinking workshop. In all these cases, at the core of the process is the concept of exploration. Individuals and teams are just way more creative and innovative the more they explore.

A very pragmatic way to conceptualize this principle is as a diamond, as depicted in Figure 2.1.

Figure 2.1 The diamond framework.

On the left of the diamond is the problem to be tackled. This is where you start by specifying the problem in a clear, succinct way. Extending out to the right, as the diamond opens up, is the divergence phase of the diamond framework. This is the place (or prompt) to explore many alternatives to solving the problem, or to "widen your options" (Heath and Heath, 2013). The goal here is to explore more options and alternatives than is comfortable or easy. Go beyond the obvious. Push yourself or your team to generate 8, 10, or 12 alternative ways to possibly address the solution. This is where creativity happens. If you keep getting locked into an obvious option, then assume that obvious option has disappeared. What would you do now? Chip and Dan Heath call this the "vanishing options test," and it works well as a mini prompt to push past cognitive lock-in.

In his book *Sprint: How to Solve Big Problems and Test New Ideas in Just Five Days*, Jake Knapp, John Zeratsky, and Braden Kowitz (2016) offer another useful prompt to inspire divergent solution exploration in the middle section of the diamond. They call it "crazy eights"—take a piece of paper and fold it in half, in half again, and in half again, so when the paper is unfolded, your creases create eight identical blocks. Next, in each block, quickly sketch a different possible solution to your identified problem. Use quick and crude sketches, compressing the available time. Give yourself only one or two minutes for each sketch. This is a rapid way to expand your solution set.

However, exploring multiple different solutions can also take time. As was illustrated in the IDEO and Away examples shared earlier, the exploration phase can take days or even weeks. If you are tackling a challenging problem, you may need time to consider and explore many different alternatives to address that problem.

Returning to the diamond framework, on the right of the diamond is the convergence phase. Once you have different options "on the table," the next step is to narrow those options. This entails reflecting on the ideas on the table and considering which are attractive based on feasibility, cost, creativity, or another marker. It may also entail combining ideas from different options to create something unique. Sketch out a few rough details for the best two or three ideas from this option set and then share them with others to get their input.

Every time I prompt entrepreneurs to explore more options in this way, they impress themselves by what they produce.

Embracing the Exploration Principle on Your Entrepreneurial Journey

What does it look and feel like to fully embrace the exploration principle to make meaningful progress in your entrepreneurial endeavor? Fully embracing the exploration principle on the entrepreneurial journey may entail the following:

- Carefully examining and learning about what currently exists in the market to solve the problem you wish to address
- Keeping a record of different options and ideas for solving the problem and keeping a notebook, taking pictures, and/or making voice memos
- Generating a large number of diverse ideas for solving the problem
- Engaging in fast and slow problem solving and pushing yourself to quickly come up with diverse solutions and also allowing time for diverse solutions to percolate and evolve
- Pushing yourself to go beyond obvious solutions and using the vanishing options test to eliminate obvious options from the option pool

Exploration is a key part of what entrepreneurs do. They identify problems and then explore novel and valuable ways to solve those problems. Being on the startup journey is like being on a treasure hunt to find the best solution to a meaningful problem, but to do that, one needs to search far and wide. Therefore, exploration is baked into entrepreneurship. But exploration leads to ideas, and ideas need to be developed. That's where the other principles of entrepreneurial progress come in. I turn to those next.

3

The Simplicity Principle

There is likely not a single person reading this book who has not heard of Instagram. Today, Instagram is a giant photo-sharing and social-networking platform owned by Facebook. As of the time of this writing, Instagram was the world's fourth-largest social media platform with 1.3 billion active users. But it did not start out that way; it started as a complex, scrappy, location-based check-in app called Burbn.

Burbn allowed users to check in at specific locations, message other users to make plans for future check-ins, earn points for hanging out with friends, and post pictures of meetups. The app had "a jumble of features that made it confusing," noted creativity researcher Keith Sawyer in an article in the *Atlantic* (Garber, 2014). Although Burbn captured some early users, most were people in the founders' network. Growth quickly stagnated with just a few hundred active users, and Burbn founders Kevin Systrom and Mike Kreiger realized something needed to change or else they'd be "dead in the water."

Kevin and Mike decided to carefully examine how people were using what they had originally created. They analyzed user data and tracked usage patterns. Their finding? People were using just one simple feature of the app. "They were posting and sharing photos like crazy," explained Sawyer in his retelling of the story (Garber, 2014).

In response, the founders stripped away everything else in the Burbn app, used the most basic technology and code, and relaunched as the simplest photo-sharing app possible. Their one key additional insight came when Kevin was on vacation with his

The Principles of Entrepreneurial Progress. Greg Fisher, Oxford University Press.
© Oxford University Press 2024. DOI: 10.1093/oso/9780197669815.003.0004

wife in Mexico around the time they were going through their re-configuration. "We rented a little room in a bed and breakfast, and I was working on Burbn at the time, and we were pivoting to photos, but she was like, 'I don't think I'm going to ever use this app.... My photos aren't good.... They're not as good as your friend Greg's.' I was like, 'Well, Greg filters all his photos.' And she looks at me, and she's like, 'Well, you should add filters then,'" recounted Kevin to Reid Hoffman on the *Masters of Scale* podcast. "I was like, 'Ah, you're right. I should add filters.'" Via the dial-up internet at the bed and breakfast in Mexico, Kevin researched how to write the code to add filters to his app. "I made the first filter there on the spot. It's still in the app, called X-Pro 2," recounted Kevin (Systrom, n.d.). It wasn't perfect, but it was simple, and it was enough to get things going.

When interviewed many years later on the *Tim Ferris Show*, Kevin said that one of his main product management, technology-scaling, and broader life philosophies is to "always do the simple thing first. It's amazing to me how many people think the quality of their management . . . is judged based on the complexity of their decisions or the outcomes. It turns out actually the *right* thing to do is sometimes the *simplest*, and it's the most effective. I live that as a value both in life and at work as well" (Systrom, 2019).

With this philosophy, Instagram scaled to 13 employees and 30 million users in just two years before being acquired by Facebook for $1 billion in 2012.

Around the time Facebook was bidding to buy Instagram, all the way across the Pacific Ocean and below the equator, Kiwi Tim Brown was stepping away from an eight-year professional soccer career that included a trip to the 2010 FIFA World Cup as New Zealand's vice captain.

With an undergraduate degree in design science from the University of Cincinnati's School of Design, Architecture, Art, and Planning, Tim had spent much of his free time (when he wasn't playing soccer) designing and developing a new sneaker with one core premise in mind: simplicity. At the time, this was just a "curiosity project" that allowed him to tinker and stay connected with his passion for design while he pursued professional sports (Brown and Zwillinger, 2019).

Throughout his playing career, Tim was often required to wear sponsored sneakers from big-name brands like Adidas and Nike. But he felt that these sneakers were too flashy, awash with too many different colors and overwhelmed with corporate logos. He wanted something simpler, much simpler. So, he played around with what they might look like and devised a single-color pair of simple sneakers made of merino wool. He even went as far as having a few prototypes developed in his off season.

Then, in 2012, with his soccer career behind him, he moved to London to pursue a graduate degree in business at the London School of Economics. While there, he used his simple "shoe idea" for a school project, leading one of his professors to challenge him to pressure test his "curiosity project" with real customers. His professor reportedly called his "wool shoe" a questionable idea and pushed Tim to test it before he wasted any more of his time on it. To test it, Tim launched a Kickstarter campaign with a video that cost just $300 to produce. To his amazement, he sold out of all his inventory—1,000 pairs—within four days. He had to halt the campaign early because he did not have enough material to fulfill orders beyond what had already been purchased (Brown and Zwillinger, 2019). Apparently, more people than just him valued his very simple sneaker aesthetic.

When Allbirds officially launched in 2016, they offered only one model, the Wool Runner sneaker, and they continue to maintain a very streamlined product line. While most other shoe manufacturers would capitalize on Allbirds' initial success by releasing a wide range of designs and colors, Tim and his cofounder Joey Zwillinger have kept things simple, really simple. Allbirds' footwear is not attention grabbing; it will not make the list of most outrageous footwear of the year. Instead, Allbirds' shoes have a minimalist look. Although it was certainly not a smooth or easy path to go from the $120,000 Kickstarter campaign to the $1.4 billion Allbirds shoe and clothing brand that we know today, the path was made more feasible and doable because they remained committed to the simplicity principle.

"I had a very, very simple insight that shoes were over-logoed, over-colored and changed all the time for no reason. It was very, very difficult to find 'simple.' And I set out to solve that," said Tim in a CNBC interview (Huddleston Jr., 2018).

The Principle

Across two very different industries—social networking versus shoes—and two contrasting types of businesses, we see how embracing simplicity empowered startup founders to make meaningful progress in their entrepreneurial journeys. However, embracing simplicity is not easy. In fact, it's downright difficult. Our natural tendency is often to make things more complex by adding and overengineering. Most people's underlying belief is that adding and making things more complex is the natural way to create and convey value.

Recent research published in the journal *Nature* reported findings from across eight different experiments exploring whether people tend to search for subtractive changes (i.e. take things away) less readily than they search for additive changes (i.e. add things in) (Adams et al., 2021). The eight experiments examined individuals' inclinations to "add to" or "subtract from" LEGO structures, miniature golf holes, and a digital grid pattern. After analyzing the data from the eight experiments, the researchers concluded that "people systematically default to searching for additive transformations, and consequently overlook subtractive transformations" (Adams et al., 2021: 258).

By consistently overlooking subtractive changes (taking stuff away), research participants neglected valuable opportunities to simplify their solutions. In his book *Subtract*, Leidy Klotz (2021) (who was also one of the authors on the *Nature* articles) shared similar insights from additional experiments in which participants intuitively added rather than subtracted as a means to improve something. They added more food to cooking recipes; they squeezed more activities into an already overfull itinerary for a day's worth of activities in Washington, DC; they inserted more notes into an already complex music composition; and they added sentences and words to an essay to try to improve it.

Our draw to make things more complex than they need to be is so strong that psychologists have even given it a name: complexity bias. On the *Farnam Street* blog, which has emerged as a great resource for credible information on different mental models, the author defines complexity bias as "our tendency to look at something that is easy to understand or look at it when we are in a state of confusion, and view it as having many parts that are difficult to understand." Simply put, "We often find it easier to face a complex problem than a simple one" (Farnam Street, n.d.).

For entrepreneurs, this tendency to add and create complexity can be very costly. Under conditions of uncertainty, ambiguity, and resource constraints, making anything more complex than it needs to be is destructive. It makes ideas difficult to communicate and complicated to execute, and it often generates a need for additional resources and time in an already constrained environment.

One of the reasons it can be tempting to make products, business models, or services needlessly more complex is because, as Steve Magnus pointed out, "We often mistake complexity with knowledge." He explained, "A recent study found that people use jargon when they lack perceived status. They are compensating. When we aren't secure in our knowledge or understanding, we complexify. When we know what we're talking about, we focus on clarity" (Magnus, n.d.). This means that if you don't deeply and intricately understand the problem you are trying to solve and aren't able to properly conceptualize the solution you intend to offer, then you are more likely to complexify what you are doing. Entrepreneurs often seek to impress with more complex solutions when simple ones are much more impactful, are easier to execute, and generate more value. As Paul Graham (2008), the founder of Y Combinator, noted, "Though simple solutions are better, they don't seem as impressive as complex ones." Simple solutions are what lead to microbursts of progress and sustained momentum in the entrepreneurial journey, yet it is often tempting to do what is more complex—to add rather than subtract.

The Simplicity Principle:
Entrepreneurial progress entails solving the identified problem as *simply as possible.*

One of the sad examples of overlooking the simplicity principle is Quirky. Quirky was initially an intriguing, well-executed idea for an invention platform developed by Ben Kaufmann to "make invention accessible." Powered by the internet, social media, and new technology, the platform enabled inventors to pitch their ideas, and if an idea was voted up by the community, the firm would fine-tune the design; manufacture the product; and manage retail partners, including Amazon, the Museum of Modern Art, Bed Bath & Beyond, and Target. Over time, Quirky raised $170 million from Norwest Venture Partners, RRE Ventures, GE Ventures, and Andreessen Horowitz.

However, Quirky's product portfolio quickly became wide, unwieldy, and disconnected, and because the team was managing so many different aspects of each different product's value chain—idea sourcing, refinement, product development, manufacturing, wholesale, and retail—there was just too much going on (Fixson and Tucker, 2016). The business was overly complex. In reporting on Quirky's ultimate demise and bankruptcy, the *New York Times* noted that "Quirky had some success, with revenue rising sharply [in 2014] to about $100 million. But the scale of its ambitions—managing a sprawling community of inventors, transforming raw ideas into product designs, and orchestrating manufacturing and distribution—proved daunting and too costly" (Lohr, 2015).

So, how might founders practically overcome complexity bias such that they can embrace the simplicity principle? That's what I turn to next.

The Practice

Experts suggest that one of the most effective tools we have for overcoming complexity bias is a concept known as Occam's razor. William of Ockham was a 14th-century friar, philosopher, and theologian, and his characteristic way of making deductions inspired the following heuristic: *the simplest explanation is preferable to one that is more complex* (Farnam Street, n.d.). Simple theories are easier to verify, and simple solutions are easier to execute. Also known as the principle of parsimony, this problem-solving principle is used to eliminate improbable options in a given situation. When we don't have enough empirical evidence to disprove a hypothesis, we should avoid making unfounded assumptions or adding unnecessary complexity so we can make quick decisions or establish truths. I recently read the book *The Great Mental Models Volume 1: General Thinking Concepts* by Shane Parrish (2019), and of all the dozen models covered in the book, Occam's razor is the one I found most memorable and impactful. It's also the one I have used most in a multitude of different situations. It is a simple prompt to cut through complexity and elicit simplicity. While some of the principles in this book apply very specifically to entrepreneurial and business scenarios (e.g., problem principle), the simplicity principle applies across a broad and wide-ranging number of scenarios in many facets of life. This is one reason I have found the chapter on simplicity in *The Great Mental Models* book to be so impactful.

Although looking for simple solutions and not complexifying startups sounds easy, it's not. It's much easier to just keep adding on layers of complexity. It takes discipline and effort to make (and keep) your venture simple. Simplicity can be embraced in various aspects of a new venture: it can be embedded in the actual product or service, it can be reflected in the internal organizational processes and structure, it can come through the adopted technology solutions, it can be reflected in the supply chain or distribution channels, it can be ingrained in the firm's business model, or it can manifest as a narrow and lean product portfolio.

So, how can you make this happen? Here are a few prompts that can lead you down the simplification path. Not all of these prompts will apply to every business concept, but it is worth responding to the ones that are relevant to your venture. They will help you think about what can possibly be stripped away to simplify what you are doing. I highly recommend that you set aside an hour or two, find a reflective place to sit (your favorite coffee shop, a quiet corner of the library, your porch or outdoor table), and write down a detailed response to as many of these prompts as possible.

- If you were forced to generate and launch a solution for the problem you seek to address in less than 24 hours, what would you do?
- If you were forced to launch your idea with only off-the-shelf technology, how would you do it?
- If you knew that you would have to launch your idea with a drastically reduced workforce, what would you do?
- If you only had one day a week to work on your venture, how would you launch your idea?
- If you were to eliminate half of your planned product or service features, what would you get rid of?

These prompts will steer you toward elements of your venture that can possibly be simplified, minimized, or eliminated to allow you to focus on what's really important: developing something that solves a real customer problem. Doing so simply will eliminate costs, increase speed, and enable you to actually get stuff done.

I recently came across this tweet by Karthik Sridharan (n.d.), an entrepreneur in India who has bootstrapped his venture Flexiple from nothing to $3 million in annual recurring revenue:

"Your startup's customer doesn't care if:
- Your tech is built on Golang or PHP
- You use AI/ML, Blockchain or execute manually
- You analyse 150 data points with Big data or run on Excel
It simply boils down to whether you are solving their problem."

The practice of simplification goes beyond just the early or initial phases of a new venture. As your venture scales, it is important to continually assess what you are doing, question whether you are doing it as simply as possible, and avoid adding anything that will increase the complexity of your business unless there is a very justifiable reason to do so.

The Tool

So, how can you guard against complexity in your startup? One way to do so is to use the SIMPLE framework described below to prompt you to think about problems, challenges, opportunities, and issues. In seeking to address a problem, challenge, opportunity, or issue—be it the core problem your venture seeks to address (as per the first principle, the problem principle) or a challenge, opportunity, or issue that arises as your venture launches and scales— use the SIMPLE acronym to evaluate how you might solve that problem simply.

Work through the SIMPLE acronym as follows:

- **S:** Subtract elements where possible. Get rid of what's not necessary or essential.
- **I:** Imitate others who have solved a similar problem or challenge. Look at what others have done to overcome a similar issue to the one you face.
- **M:** Minimize features in what you are developing. Almost all products and services are developed with more features than users can and will use, so get rid of features that are not critical.
- **P:** Prune products in your product portfolio. Focus on developing fewer products rather than more. Each additional product you develop adds significant complexity to your entity.
- **L:** Leverage resources that you already control and/or resources that are already developed, such as off-the-shelf technology solutions. In other words, utilize what already exists when solving challenges or addressing issues.
- **E:** Edit your explanations and descriptions of what you are doing and how you convey them to others.

The SIMPLE acronym is a method to help enact the simplicity principle. There are other ways to focus on doing what is most simple, but the SIMPLE acronym, as depicted in Figure 3.1, is a way to prompt you to think about it in the context of developing and scaling an entrepreneurial venture.

Fully Embracing the Simplicity Principle on Your Entrepreneurial Journey

What does it look like and feel like to fully embrace the simplicity principle so you can make meaningful progress in your

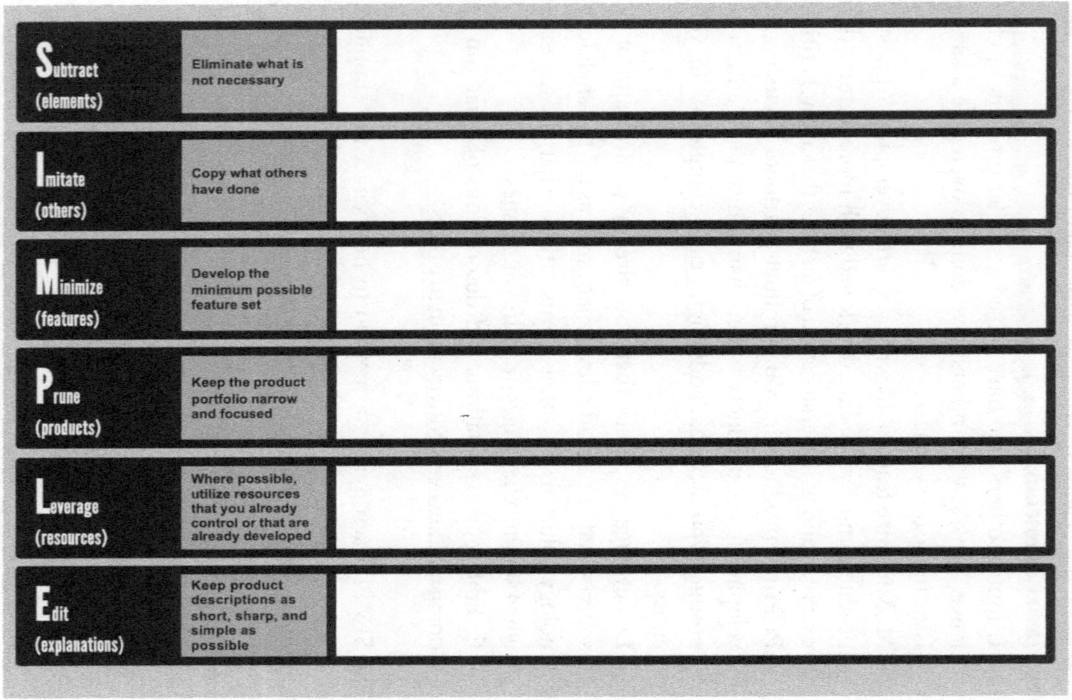

Subtract (elements)	Eliminate what is not necessary
Imitate (others)	Copy what others have done
Minimize (features)	Develop the minimum possible feature set
Prune (products)	Keep the product portfolio narrow and focused
Leverage (resources)	Where possible, utilize resources that you already control or that are already developed
Edit (explanations)	Keep product descriptions as short, sharp, and simple as possible

Figure 3.1 The SIMPLE framework for reducing complexity.

entrepreneurial endeavor? Fully embracing the simplicity principle in the entrepreneurial journey may entail the following:

- Addressing each problem, issue, challenge, or opportunity as simply as possible
- Carefully assessing what can be eliminated or reduced to streamline what you do
- Conceiving of a product with as few features as possible so you can easily build the first version
- Aiming to have a very narrow set of products even as you scale the business
- Explaining what you do quickly and easily in very simple terms

In contrast, the following may indicate that you are overlooking or ignoring the simplicity principle:

- Just adding in layers of complexity to solve each issue that arises
- Never thinking carefully about what you might eliminate or reduce to streamline what you do
- Conceiving of a feature-rich product that will be very difficult to build
- Aiming to have a very broad set of products in a very short space of time
- Engaging in long, detailed explanations to describe what you do

4

The Prototype Principle

Many experts will say you should not try to pursue a venture when you don't personally have the skills needed to bring it to life. A communications professional shouldn't get into finance, a health care worker shouldn't get into coding, and a ballerina shouldn't get into tech.

Yet, Brynn Putnam, a former New York City Ballet ballerina, created *Mirror*, a fitness technology company that was sold to Lululemon in 2020 for $500 million, just four years after it was founded and just two years after the product was launched.

As a teenager, Brynn was accepted into the New York City Ballet and, almost synchronously, also accepted into Harvard. She would go on to do both, balancing what she called her analytical and creative self to achieve both her professional and personal aspirations.

After leaving the New York City Ballet, Brynn could not find a fitness option that met her needs as an athlete. As a result, she created Refine Method, an exercise studio with instructor-led classes that utilize resistance training and cardio workouts to challenge participants in unique ways. The classes were a near-instant hit, and Brynn would later expand to three studio locations in New York City (CNBC, 2021).

Six years later and pregnant with her first child, Brynn was not slowing down in her professional ambition, but physically, she found it difficult to continue her regular rigorous studio-based workouts as her body and hormones changed. The idea of going to the studio was becoming less and less appealing. Knowing there were many others who were averse to going to a fitness studio to work out, she began to consider other alternatives (CNBC, 2021).

The Principles of Entrepreneurial Progress. Greg Fisher, Oxford University Press.
© Oxford University Press 2024. DOI: 10.1093/oso/9780197669815.003.0005

How could she meet her own need for an at-home fitness option and provide quality options for others with a similar desire to work out in the privacy of their homes?

She began to analyze the at-home workout experience. Among the myriad options, she discovered a common issue in the form of a lack of an accountability system: there was nothing to get you started or keep you going outside of self-motivation. Additionally, the onus of providing equipment fell to the athlete—equipment was typically expensive, large, and visually disruptive to the aesthetic of a room. This was particularly problematic in New York City, where most people's apartments are small and living and storage space comes at a premium. To Brynn, all the current options for at-home fitness seemed like a poor substitute for in-person instruction rather than a sustainable and enjoyable long-term solution (Putnam, 2020).

How could she give her members the same value of an in-person class with the ease of an at-home workout? How could she conquer the at-home fitness solutions market when it was rife with unattractive and expensive equipment? Could it even be done?

While Brynn was considering the answer to this, she remembered she had recently installed full-length mirrors in her fitness studios to rave reviews from clients. The visual feedback inspired members to work harder and to improve their form all at once. This led to the "of course" moment—what if the solution to Brynn's at-home workout was a mirror? But instead of a "dumb" mirror, what if it could be connected to provide users with visual cues, feedback, and other forms of instruction and accountability? (Putnam, 2020).

Her reaction wasn't to go and hire an engineering firm to design and build a concept or to take her idea to a big company that might offer to develop the idea as her partner. Either of those options would have likely led to many obstacles and challenges; long, unproductive meetings; hearing "no" much more than "yes"; and making very little (if any) progress toward bringing her idea to life.

Instead of drowning in red tape, Brynn kept momentum by building a crude prototype of what she had conceived.

The first prototype was the definition of crude: a cheap tablet from Amazon, a piece of glass, and a Raspberry Pi (a small low-cost computer often used by do-it-yourself [DYI] hobbyists). She used YouTube videos and other DIY instructions to pull the concept together (Ruffner, 2018). It wasn't pretty (at all), but it worked. Brynn recounted that the initial prototype was not functional in terms of being interactive or being able to coach a user through a workout. Essentially, it just showed an image through a standard mirror, but even this modest iteration led to valuable learning (Putnam, 2020). Interestingly, she also built another non-working prototype that looked sleek and beautiful to illustrate what the end product could look like and highlight how it would fit seamlessly into a home.

With both a crude, semifunctional prototype and a sleek, beautiful prototype in hand, she secured her first round of funding. Even as a solo founder with very little startup experience and no technology background, she managed to convince investors that Mirror was a worthy bet. One reason she could successfully do this was because she had built those various prototypes, which allowed investors to see the vision of Mirror and interact with the "product" in a way that a standard pitch or a paper drawing just couldn't do. This product would quickly go on to garner praise from famous first movers like Alicia Keys, Ellen DeGeneres, Gwyneth Paltrow, and Jennifer Aniston. Less than five years after Brynn developed those initial prototypes, Lululemon acquired Mirror for more than $500 million (CNBC, 2021).

While many things have contributed to the success of Mirror, certainly one key ingredient is Brynn's willingness and inclination to rapidly prototype her idea and to develop different iterations of that prototype to methodically test different aspects of its appeal.

The Principle

A prototype is an early sample, model, or release of a product or service built to test a concept or process. It is a term used in a variety of contexts, including design, product development, and software programming. In entrepreneurship, a prototype is sometimes referred to as a minimum viable product (MVP)—an early version of a product with just enough features to be usable by early customers, who can then provide feedback for future product development.

Building a prototype of a product or service typically involves much less cost, time, and effort than building the final product, yet it allows a creator to generate a concrete depiction of their idea before making further investments in developing that concept. It might entail creating a mockup of a website or app before doing all the web design and development to produce the fully working, well-designed version. It might entail assembling a version of the product using relatively inexpensive, immediately accessible off-the-shelf elements and components, as Brynn did with Mirror. It might entail acting out a service process to reflect the intended flow and interconnecting linkages between different elements of the process.

In the process of writing this book, I decided to embrace the prototype principle. Soon after coming up with the idea for the book, I penned a long blog post, covering and sharing key ideas that I envisaged would be part of the book. I organized my ideas in a way that is not that different from how this book is organized, and I even did some high-level research on some of the stories that are now part of the book. After having my editor look over the post, I uploaded it to LinkedIn and shared it with those in my LinkedIn network, and I allowed them to share it more broadly with their personal networks.

As with building any prototype, the process of prototyping this book allowed me to make progress and create momentum in a few very meaningful ways. First, it forced me to take immediate action toward the end goal that I desired. Without developing a prototype, I would most likely have just continued to think, dream, and talk about writing a book, but I wouldn't have started actually writing.

Second, it allowed me to learn critical things about the process of developing the end product. I gained a deeper understanding of how easy or difficult it was to research certain types of stories. By seeing everything laid out as a prototype, I was able to experiment with different ways of organizing the material. A draft prototype also helped me learn how long it might take to write a 3,000-word chapter, which helped me budget my time over the proceeding days, weeks, and months. Learning is accelerated and deepened through doing and building a prototype prompts one to learn through doing.

Third, building a prototype allowed me to share my ideas in a concrete form and to assess my audience's reactions to what I had developed. Not only was I able to assess the general reactions of those in my LinkedIn network to my ideas about the *Principles of Entrepreneurial Progress*, but I was also able to evaluate other important considerations: Who reacted? Which audience groups do these ideas resonate with? Are they the same audience groups I am targeting? Furthermore, I could share those reactions with publishers to get them to support the endeavor.

These three factors—action, learning, and reaction—are three big reasons that prototyping is so valuable. Building a prototype spurs action, facilitates learning, and generates valuable reactions from others to one's ideas.

The Prototype Principle:

Entrepreneurial progress entails *rapidly building a prototype* of the identified solution.

A Managerial Mindset versus a
Design Mindset

People with a managerial mindset often find it difficult to prototype, or it does not even cross their minds as a viable path forward. In Jeanne Liedtka and Tim Ogilvie's (2011) book *Designing for Growth*, they wrote, "As a manager, you are probably more adept at thinking without drawing or prototyping. But you are not adept at helping others see your thoughts. That's why you must prototype—to make your thoughts explicit so that others can grasp them quickly and share their thoughts with you" (142).

Across the many entrepreneurs I have studied (some of them featured in this book), those who make meaningful progress in bringing a new idea to light embrace a "design mindset" over a "managerial mindset." Instead of thinking about how they might control and coordinate things from a distance, they get into the action and start creating. The core of a design mindset is building prototypes—making things, trying things, taking action, and getting ideas out of your head and into concrete form.

Building crude prototypes is one of the things that business school students often find extremely challenging when they are first encouraged to do it, but it is one of the things that they find most powerful, most revealing, and most valuable once they have done it. It's a bit like going for a walk or a run. You resist it before you do it, actually quite enjoy it while you are doing it, and are extremely grateful that you did it afterward. Business school tends to be more about abstract concepts and theoretical ideas, but prototyping prompts a shift from the abstract to the concrete, from the theoretical to the real. This shift is very meaningful. It generates real momentum.

The Practice and the Tool

How does one decide what prototype to build? Is there a sensible way to build a series of prototypes over time? How do you use a prototype once it is built?

One way to think about variation in a prototype is in terms of the prototype's fidelity. Fidelity is the degree of exactness with which something is produced, copied, or reproduced, and a prototype can vary from low to high fidelity. A high-fidelity prototype is very close to what the intended product will look like and how it will work. It is produced with a high degree of exactness to the desired product or service. Conversely, a low-fidelity prototype is much less refined or functional.

As illustrated by the Mirror example, a prototype can be distinguished broadly on whether it encapsulates functional or aesthetic elements of the intended product or service. A functional prototype shows how the product or service is meant to work, and the higher it is in functional fidelity, the closer it is to fully functioning as intended. An aesthetic prototype shows how the product or service is meant to look, and the higher it is in aesthetic fidelity, the closer it is to its intended final aesthetic form.

A prototype that is developed to be high in both functional fidelity and aesthetic fidelity will be very close to the intended version of the product or service being developed. However, such a prototype will also take significant time, effort, energy, and resources to develop. Therefore, the intention in an entrepreneurial endeavor is not to start with a prototype that is high in both functional fidelity and aesthetic fidelity. Instead, it makes sense to start out developing a prototype that is low in both functional fidelity and aesthetic fidelity that can be made quickly and easily. Then, the learning from that experience can be used to make additional prototypes that increase in functional and/or aesthetic fidelity, thereby progressively working toward developing a prototype that is closer to the intended product or service.

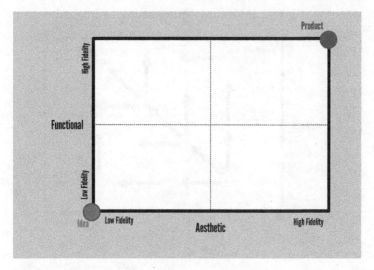

Figure 4.1 The prototype matrix.

The prototype development options and pathways can be nicely depicted on a 2 × 2 matrix with functional and aesthetic fidelity on each axis and low fidelity and high fidelity at the extreme ends of each axis, as depicted in Figure 4.1.

On the bottom-left corner of the matrix is the initial product or service idea before it is converted into any kind of prototype, and on the top-right corner is the fully developed intended product or service, where the full functionality and aesthetics of the intended product are evident.

The opportunity for a founder is to navigate their way from an idea toward a product or service by building various prototypes in different areas of this matrix, starting in the bottom left and progressing to the top right, as depicted in Figure 4.2.

To navigate a path from an idea to a fully functioning, beautiful product or service, certain questions can prompt action and thus generate microbursts of entrepreneurial progress at different stages of product development.

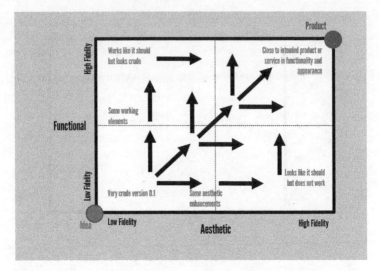

Figure 4.2 The prototype matrix with pathways toward creating a product.

Very early in the product development process, ask the following:

- What can I build quickly and crudely?
- How can I transform my idea into something concrete as soon as possible?
- Do I need different types of prototypes to test and show different aspects of the solution (e.g., functionality, aesthetics, fit within a broader ecosystem)?

Then, after developing a few early prototypes, ask the following:

- How can I evolve my product (or service) prototypes to learn more?
- Should I shift toward a prototype that is higher in functional fidelity, aesthetic fidelity, or both?

- What have I learned from earlier prototypes that might inform how I develop my next prototypes?

Much of the power of the prototype principle comes from actually building the prototype. As an entrepreneur, you can learn about your product or service and the nuances of developing it by building an initial version of it. But beyond that, you can also share a prototype with venture stakeholders—including prospective customers, suppliers, partners, or investors—to get their feedback and input on what you are trying to do. As mentioned earlier, Brynn Putnam of Mirror shared two prototypes—a functional but ugly one and a beautiful but nonfunctional one—with venture capital investors, and it was these prototypes that helped convince them to invest in Mirror. Sharing prototypes with prospective customers is also very powerful—it allows you to get meaningful feedback from your target audience about the direction you are taking with your offering. This is what is preached in the lean startup approach of Eric Ries and Steve Blank where entrepreneurs are pushed to follow the build-measure-learn cycle, which entails (1) building a prototype, (2) exposing it to customers and measuring their reaction, and (3) learning from their reaction such that you can then build a new, more refined, and more appealing prototype and go through the whole cycle again.

Creating a series of prototypes provides a level of learning and insight about a new venture that is mostly unattainable from other sources. Prototypes are a natural, efficient, and effective way to learn about product development, design, supplier and value chain options, customer preferences, and business model alternatives under conditions of uncertainty, ambiguity, and resource constraints. However, to amplify the impact of enacting the prototype principle, it is incredibly valuable to combine and integrate it with many of the other principles discussed in this book, especially the experimentation and iteration principles that I discuss next.

5

The Experimentation Principle

Cutting back on alcohol consumption. This is the problem Bill Shufelt was trying to solve back in 2015. He had recently stopped drinking in preparation to run an ultramarathon, and he felt great—he slept more soundly, lost weight, and had more energy overall. He wanted to keep limiting his alcohol intake even after the run, but he often found himself in situations where the ritual and taste of a beer seemed so fitting.

"Why are there no great-tasting alcohol-free beers?" he wondered.

Across the United States and globally, there had been a revolution in craft brewing—smaller independent breweries creating flavorful, rich, complex beers in small batches. While craft brewing enabled an explosion of new brands on the market, notably, there had been no new alcohol-free beers launched since the early 1990s, and most beer drinkers squirmed at the thought of drinking an alcohol-free beer. "It was like being put in the penalty box," explained Bill. "The only options were flavorless, watery, metallic in taste, and came with punchlines of decades-old jokes" (Shufelt, 2020).

He decided to try to tackle the problem.

Bill began consuming textbooks on weekends and learning about the process of brewing beer in the evenings. He discovered that for alcohol-free beer, the typical process was to remove alcohol after the brewing process was complete. But this process was complex, and it put a ceiling on achievable quality and taste. He began to apply the principles of brewing to conceive of a way to eradicate alcohol as part of the brewing process instead of adding

The Principles of Entrepreneurial Progress. Greg Fisher, Oxford University Press.
© Oxford University Press 2024. DOI: 10.1093/oso/9780197669815.003.0006

an additional step postbrew that strips the mixture of much of the flavor.

However, he soon realized that he did not have the experience to refine this process and deploy it at scale. He set out to find a partner, but finding interested parties was tough. Bill contacted more than 200 brewers across the United States to gauge their interest and see if they would be willing to partner in experimenting on his alcohol-free craft beer project.

"There was no market for non-alcoholic beer in the US," Bill said. "The non-alcoholic beer market hadn't seen any new products in 20 to 30 years. . . . The category hadn't grown for 15 years" (Shufelt, 2020). To the brewers, this looked like a nonexistent opportunity, but to Bill, the market was underserved and lacking innovation. He *knew* customers were out there—he was one of them. And he knew there were even more people like him.

"[Alcohol-free beer] really fits well with the modern, healthy lifestyle," he said. Why couldn't other brewers see the opportunity that seemed so obvious to him?

John Walker was one of the most decorated brewers Bill talked to, winning both national and international awards for his craft brews, and the only one to see potential in Bill's vision. After a few conversations about Bill's vision, John believed so wholeheartedly in the project that he decided to move out of Santa Fe, New Mexico, and join Bill in Connecticut to start Athletic Brewing Company.

Together, Bill and John faced the challenge, as many entrepreneurs do, of creating something entirely new. Their goal was to create great-tasting alcohol-free craft beer using a never-before-tried brewing method, and to meet that challenge, their superpower was experimentation. They had some basic ideas of how they might get started thanks to the many hours of research Bill had done, but they ended up brewing "over 100 batches on homebrew equipment to perfect our process," said Bill. "Through hundreds of trials, tweaking natural variables like temperature, we found that with about 12 to 15 changes to the normal brewing process, we could brew super sessionable beer that was fully fermented and conditioned to under 0.5% ABV" (Salazar, 2020).

Initially, it was just the two founders tasting the outcomes of their experiments, but as things evolved, they shared their experimental brews more broadly, eventually launching their nonalcoholic IPA and Golden Ale brews for sale under the Athletic Brewing brand (Athletic Brewing, n.d.).

Just two years after launching, they were producing more than 40,000 barrels of beer per year, and all of that was still not enough to keep up with demand. At the time of writing, they had raised $50 million in capital to expand their facilities to try to keep up with demand (Fooddive, 2021). All this would not have happened if they did not first experiment.

The Principle

Entrepreneurship is about doing new things or doing familiar things in new ways. It is about introducing something novel to one's ecosystem. However, regardless of all the planning, testing, and projecting involved, it is seldom clear upfront whether a new product or service is going to work. To overcome the uncertainty and ambiguity of novelty and newness, founders benefit immensely from adopting the predilections of a scientist to experiment and figure out a viable and appealing path forward. Experimentation is the act or process of trying out new ideas, methods, or activities to learn and develop new knowledge and insights.

Experimentation entails shifting from conjecture or intuition to action, documentation, and results followed by an analysis of those results. The goal is to learn things from those results that one could not learn in any other way. It is an action-oriented way to learn, much like the prototype principle in this sense.

Research supports the notion that experimentation makes a positive impact in the entrepreneurial journey. Researchers at Bocconi

University conducted a randomized controlled experiment involving 116 early-stage Italian startups divided into a treatment group and a control group. The entrepreneurs in the treatment group were trained to think and act like scientists—to experiment. They were trained to collect evidence through robustly designed experiments and rigorous data analysis (Camuffo et al., 2020). The entrepreneurs in the control group were only trained in more traditional business concepts.

The researchers discovered that the founders in the treatment group who had been trained to experiment were less likely to stick with ideas that didn't ultimately work out. In particular, they found that the "entrepreneurs who were taught to formulate hypotheses from theories and rigorously test them on carefully chosen samples of potential customers were more likely to acknowledge that an idea was bad, pivot from non-starters or pitfalls, and generate more revenue than the control group," as reported in *Harvard Business Review* by Spina, Camuffo, and Gambardella (2020). In essence, the entrepreneurs who were taught to experiment were more likely to do so (no surprise) but were much better off for doing so (which is important).

Experimentation can be used to figure out different aspects of an entrepreneurial venture. The most obvious place to experiment in the early phases of the entrepreneurial journey is with respect to the product or service. Here, one can experiment to assess whether a product prototype can be built and whether it has appeal with target customers. But other areas where a founder can experiment include a venture's business model; customer segments; recruitment tactics; pitch design; and marketing messages, channels, and processes. Each of these elements can have a significant impact on the trajectory and success of a new venture, and each is uncertain when launching a new venture. By experimenting and monitoring the impact of each adjustment, a founder can more easily figure out the right path forward. Each time you experiment and learn something new, you are making meaningful entrepreneurial progress—even if the outcome of an experiment is negative.

The Experimentation Principle:
Entrepreneurial progress entails *experimenting to get stakeholder feedback* on possible solutions.

Even though experimentation can be beneficial, it can also go too far. At some point, it is also important to commit to a general template or approach that has been found to be viable. Experimentation can become an excuse for not actually making tough decisions or tradeoffs, and if it persists, it can result in an overly complex business over time.

In a research project examining ventures entering new markets, two professors—Rory McDonald from Harvard Business School and Kathy Eisenhardt from Stanford—interviewed more than 200 entrepreneurs and innovators who attempted to enter new markets to varying degrees of success (McDonald and Eisenhardt, 2020). As reported in *Harvard Business Review* (Eisenhardt and McDonald, 2020), the professors discovered that those who successfully entered a new market "test[ed] relentlessly—but then commit[ed]." They "didn't just test and learn. They used that learning to choose a single template for creating and capturing value and spent scarce resources *only* on it" (80–81). The "less-successful enterprises either committed without testing (often missing out on more lucrative opportunities) or flitted among several templates, hedging their bets without making a choice" (81).

Eisenhardt and McDonald (2020) offered a cautionary example of a firm that appeared to "over-experiment"—Evernote. They pointed out that Evernote "started as an elegant note-taking app but tried to spin into a lifestyle brand after strong interest from investors. The company built a chat app, a recipe app, a contact-management app, and a flashcard app, splitting itself along two very different business model paths: apps with a freemium model (basic product offered for free, enticing users to become paying customers for a higher-end version) and online sales of goods. Although Evernote lives on, it failed to live up to expectations"

(81–82). Evernote started with a strong, useful concept, but the company's excessive experimentation and lack of commitment to a simple value proposition and business model for creating and capturing value derailed it. So, experimentation can help a new venture make valuable progress, but too much experimentation with no commitment can cause a venture to spin out of control.

The Practice and the Tool

How does one go about implementing and utilizing the experimentation principle in a new venture setting? Because experimentation has been all the rage in the startup world lately, there are lots of different ways to adopt an experimental approach to entrepreneurship. I have looked at many of these. Some work well, but some are confusing or overwhelming, while still others are too vague to be useful. Here, I describe a simple yet robust set of steps to engage in entrepreneurial experimentation.

Step 1: Establish the most critical key uncertainties (risks) for your venture. Experiments need to test something; they need a focus. The most critical things to focus on are the aspects of a venture that are highly uncertain yet will have a big impact on the trajectory and outcome of the venture. Clark Gilbert and Matthew Eyring (2010) called these "deal-killer" and "path-dependent" risks. Deal-killer risks are uncertainties that, if left unresolved, could undermine an entire venture; they often take the form of unwarranted or underexamined assumptions. For example, a deal-killer risk for an online used bicycle retail business is whether target consumers are even inclined to purchase bikes via a website. Path-dependent risks pertain to key decisions that are based on other decisions. They are often framed as "if this, then that." The risk relates to pursuing the wrong path, which would involve wasting large sums of money, time, or both. For the online used bicycle retail business, a path-dependent risk may relate to the types of bikes that are most likely to be purchased online—in other words, the product mix of bicycles offered by the business.

The key here is for entrepreneurs to identify and document what they perceive to be the deal-killer and path-dependent risks for their ventures. One valuable way of concretizing such risks is to *specify what needs to be true to mitigate or avoid a risk* (Lafley et al., 2012). For example, for the online used bicycle retail business to mitigate the deal-killer risk, there needs to be a customer group that is readily willing to buy a used bicycle online. If such a group cannot be found, then the idea is not worth pursuing in its current form. Assuming there is a group willing to purchase used bikes online (e.g., experienced riders, mostly male, between the ages of 18 and 35), then the business needs to specify the path-dependent risk regarding which type of used bikes the target users are most likely to buy online: higher-end versus lower-end bikes, mountain versus road versus commuting bikes, gently used versus well-used bikes, etc.

Step 2: Design an experiment to gather data on the key uncertainties. The next step is to design a test to assess the key uncertainties for your venture. Here, it is critical to go beyond just asking people what they think or how they plan to act. A survey is not enough.

Create a situation where you can see and analyze how people behave in relation to your value proposition. This often entails utilizing your product or service prototype and creating an experiment where people's reactions to the prototype can be captured and assessed. If the key uncertainty is customer oriented, place a product prototype in front of potential customers and see if they react and behave in the way you intend. If the key uncertainty is finding the right supplier or partner, attempt to forge a connection with a supplier or partner such that you can see if there is even a chance to work with them. If the key uncertainty is more path dependent, you may consider running an A-B test where you compare two versions of something to figure out which performs better.

As you design a test, consider and specify what metrics you will capture and assess: what exactly are you going to measure? Most times, it makes sense for those metrics to be quantitative, but in some cases, you may complement them with qualitative data. As you specify your key metrics, also specify (before you conduct the test) what metrics reflect a successful versus unsuccessful outcome. Also consider the timing of the test. How long will it run? Does the timing impact the results? For example, running a test just prior to Christmas or running a test over a very long or very short period may skew the results. There is no golden rule for length of study or time of year to test, but consider how your choices may impact your results and adjust as needed.

You can use an experimentation plan to set up an experiment in the broader context of what you are trying to achieve in your venture. Such a plan entails first reflecting on the broader vision for a new product or service and then specifying the critical assumptions or uncertainties pertaining to that product or service. Next, a brief description of a prototype can be used to run an experiment and determine the target audience for the experiment. Thereafter, with this information as background, there is an opportunity to describe the specifics of the experiment and the conditions or experimental outcomes under which you will iterate (change things up) or persevere (stay the course), as depicted in Figure 5.1.

Step 3: Conduct an experiment to get data about the key uncertainties. Carry out the test as you have designed it. However, not all tests work out exactly as planned. You may need to adjust and adapt aspects of the test as you see how things play out. You will almost always learn something new while conducting a test even before analyzing any data. Be open to this type of learning and keep track of surprises and insights that emerge as you go.

Be advised: don't make premature decisions based on just a few data points. I have fallen into the trap of getting a few negative responses to a prototype for a new service from the first few people who experienced it, and I immediately thought it was worthless

Figure 5.1 The experimentation plan.

and shut down the test before allowing it to play out as designed. I decided based on too small of a sample size. It was only a few weeks later, when retracing what had happened and trying to figure out why we had not made progress, that I realized I had cut things short before having the full picture. A larger sample of responses led to a different insight into the new concept that was much more workable.

Step 4: Analyze the results. Gather the data from conducting your test and analyze it objectively. Analyze the data in accordance with the metrics and thresholds you established when designing the test. I find it useful to put myself in the position of an objective outsider when analyzing results. For example, analyze the data as if you were asked to do so for a class assignment: what would the recommendation be? Almost any test result can be manipulated to make it tell the story you need it to tell, but your real responsibility here is to try to interpret the data objectively and decide what to do next based on an objective analysis.

Step 5: Experiment again. Experimentation is an iterative process. It is highly unlikely that the first experiment you conduct will give you all the insights you need. Entrepreneurial progress comes from learning, and learning comes from multiple rounds of experimentation.

If the results of the experiment don't inform what your next steps should be, something went wrong. At the very least, the experiment should tell you, "Don't do that again." Preferably, the results should suggest the next experiment to perform, or they might indicate that the uncertainty is now "less risky" and it's time to investigate another element of your business model. If no clear step is apparent, it's a warning sign that you may have been experimenting on something irrelevant or low priority.

The entrepreneurial journey entails developing multiple prototypes that can be used for multiple rounds of experimentation such that you actively manage the risks inherent in your new venture. Gilbert and Eyring point out that effective entrepreneurs are good at managing risks through experimentation: "Despite stereotypes to the contrary, the best entrepreneurs are relentless about managing risks—indeed, that's their core competency. . . . Risks should be uncovered and hedged. . . . All new ventures are partly wrong and partly right. Run small, cheap, fast experiments to determine which bits are which and what course corrections you need to make" (Gilbert and Eyring, 2010: 95).

6

The Iteration Principle

I recently saw a *Bloomberg News* headline that read, "How Melanie Perkins Became the World's Richest Self-Made Female Billionaire under the Age of 40." Of all the billionaires in the world in 2021, only 12.9% were women. And somehow Melanie ranks at the top of the list at an age when many of us are only just beginning to diversify our investments or save for retirement. How did she do it?

Melanie didn't hit her big break right away. In fact, she started her first business selling handmade scarves when she was 14 and quickly latched on to the entrepreneurial allure. That excitement of creating something new and being swept up in the speed of business whetted her palate to the possibility of one day creating something bigger and better.

While in college studying communication in Perth, Western Australia, Melanie realized how difficult and inefficient it was to use existing desktop publishing software. She told Guy Raz on the *How I Built This* podcast:

> It seemed completely silly that you would take so many instruction manuals and so many steps to do the most basic of things. Students would take a whole semester just learning where the buttons were, let alone learn to design something. It seemed very apparent that this whole desktop-based thing would be completely archaic and outdated in the future. And so I had this very oversized vision for taking on all these different industries, from Microsoft Office and lots and lots of other industries as well. Rather than people using things like clipart, they should be able to have access to beautiful templates like designers do. But at

The Principles of Entrepreneurial Progress. Greg Fisher, Oxford University Press.
© Oxford University Press 2024. DOI: 10.1093/oso/9780197669815.003.0007

that point in time, I was 19, and I had no business experience, and so rather than trying to take on the entire world of design and all these really big companies, we decided to take on school yearbooks in Australia (Perkins, 2021).

Melanie dropped out of the University of Western Australia to get Fusion Books off the ground in 2007 with her cofounder Cliff Obrect. Over the next five years, it would become the largest yearbook company in Australia. The company is still expanding and is now available in both France and New Zealand.

Even though Melanie and Cliff were quite successful is their school yearbook–printing business, they did not get locked in. They used the learning from that experience to iterate toward a much bigger opportunity in online design. The yearbooks were a steppingstone to get them to the next level, but to do that, they needed to iterate and adapt. They iterated their concept, they iterated their business model, and they changed their funding structure.

Melanie created a plan to pursue what she and Cliff knew was the bigger opportunity. She flew from Australia to Silicon Valley to pitch her idea to US venture capitalists (VCs). For many months, she sought out VCs to invest in her bigger vision. She even learned to kite surf to gain extra opportunities to pitch her idea after she discovered many VCs use this as a way to network with founders. She was invited to a unique VC conference in Maui, where attendees would discuss venture opportunities in the morning and kite surf in the afternoon. Her persistence paid off, and her plan to pivot from school yearbooks to online design was funded.

The venture is known as Canva.

Even if you aren't a trained designer, it's likely you've heard of the name Canva because it was specifically designed for the "nondesigner" in mind. Utilizing a library of premade templates for social media graphics and presentations, the Canva graphic design platform allows users to easily add shapes, change colors, color-tint photos, and add text to beautiful graphics that can be shared or printed for personal or business use. The company utilizes a freemium model in which paid subscribers have access to additional design functionality. Canva's mission is to "empower everyone in the world to design anything and publish anywhere" (Canva, n.d.).

Canva was founded in 2013, and it has grown from nothing to a valuation exceeding $40 billion in 2022. That's what makes Melanie Perkins "the world's richest self-made female billionaire under the age of 40," as per the *Bloomberg News* headline. If Melanie Perkins and Cliff Obrecht had not iterated and adapted their venture vision from school yearbooks to the broader opportunity in online design, they would not have generated the foundation for the business that Canva is today.

Iteration and adaptation are an integral part of entrepreneurship. Adaptation in biology is defined as "a change or the process of change by which an organism or species becomes better suited to its environment." In entrepreneurship, adaptation is a change by which a venture becomes better suited to its environment through iteration. It is a shift that allows a venture to become more relevant.

Successful entrepreneurs iterate and adapt what they are doing all the time. Sometimes, iteration entails radical shifts in an alternate direction—large pivots from one business concept to another, from one market to another, or from one business model to another.

For example, YouTube was initially created as a dating website that would allow users to upload videos in their dating profiles, but the founders recognized that users liked the video upload feature more than any of the dating functionality (The Guardian, 2016). They then transformed the venture from a dating website to the video-hosting website we know today. Instagram (referenced in Chapter 3) was first a location check-in app called Burbn, but founders Systrom and Kreiger were responsive to data highlighting that the photo-sharing aspect of the check-in app was what really appealed to users (Garber, 2014). Slack, the now popular internal enterprise communication tool, was initially just an in-house communication technology for Glitch, an online gaming company led by Stewart Butterfield. When Glitch was failing to get traction, however, Butterfield was willing to iterate to explore other options. The big pivot here was away from online gaming and toward developing the company's internal communication tool as an external-facing product.

Other times, iteration entails more incremental adjustments where just one aspect of a product, distribution channel, marketing message, or business model is adapted. For example, in creating Mirror, Brynn Putnam needed to consistently adapt product specs to create a design that would appeal to customers at a reasonable manufacturing price point. She even ended up delaying the product launch to allow for the final few product iterations prior to public release.

The Principle

Making progress in the entrepreneurial journey is about learning, learning, learning.

The prototype principle and experimentation principle discussed earlier help founders learn a great deal about a new idea, concept, or initiative. Founders can learn about what it takes to create a product or service (prototype principle) and about initial market reactions to that product or service (experimentation principle).

But all that learning counts for nothing if nothing changes in response to what is learned. That's why founders need to iterate and adapt. They need to look for opportunities to change what they are developing in response to feedback from customers, suppliers, or other stakeholders. The objective is to switch things up to remain relevant.

Consider Melanie's entrepreneurial journey again through this lens. She started her foray into entrepreneurship with her handmade scarves. Was this a waste of time because it didn't make her a billionaire? Absolutely not. Melanie was able to learn about pricing, demand, quality control, and customer support by selling her scarves. Then, when she founded Fusion Books with Cliff, was that a waste because it was a beta version of what Canva could be in the future? No again. Melanie learned how to incorporate a business, how to work with a cofounder, how to manage sales, and how to market her produces and services. Every step of the journey was a valuable lesson in business. However, what really propelled Melanie and Cliff to the top was their ability to iterate.

The Iteration Principle:
Entrepreneurial progress entails *iterating a solution* in response to stakeholder feedback.

This might seem obvious. You're probably wondering why I am even taking the time to spell it out. *Obviously, founders need to iterate and change*, you are likely thinking to yourself. The reality is that even though it is so obvious, founders don't do it. They resist it; they resist adapting and changing even when they get negative feedback about what they are doing.

You see, our ideas, our concepts, and our ventures are extensions of who we are—parts of our identity. Research by Matthew Grimes (2018) highlights how founders become psychologically attached to their ideas. His research reflects how founders strongly identify with their initial ideas and how, as a result, they find it difficult to let go of some of those ideas and make necessary changes even when all the external signals blatantly suggest that an adjustment is necessary. Iterating an idea and adapting it to fit with what has been learned is both *obvious and difficult*. Founders often find rational reasons to avoid it.

So, what allows some founders to iterate and adapt what they are doing in response to external feedback? Some of my colleagues and I have explored this, and we have identified that founders are more likely to iterate what they are doing in response to negative external feedback if they have access to and *engage with a startup mentor*, if they are part of a *larger founding team*, and if they have *prior entrepreneurial experience* (Burnell, Stevenson, and Fisher, 2023). These factors facilitate a broader perspective for founders, allowing them to see their ventures more objectively, thereby realizing that there may be value in iterating. If you don't have access to any of these mechanisms that enable iteration (i.e., a mentor or a team) or if you are working on your first venture, then there is a valuable question you can ask yourself to ensure you capture that broader perspective: *if this was my best friend's business and they received feedback on their business similar to the feedback I have just received, what would I advise them to do?*

If you are honest in answering this question and you act on what you uncover, then you are way more likely to avoid the trap of psychological ownership and overidentification with your ideas. You are more likely to iterate.

The Practice and the Tool

When does one iterate? The short answer to this is when things are not working as they should. There are two broad reasons things may not work out as they should. The first is that the product or service that you initially conceived has *not* found product-market fit—the product or service that you envisaged does not appear to meet and satisfy a clear, strong, and obvious market demand. In other words, the assumptions you originally had about the needs of users in the market are not holding true as you expose early versions of your product or service to those potential users. Therefore, you need to revisit those assumptions and change something in the business to find that product-market fit.

The second reason you may need to iterate when building and scaling a new venture is that the external environment in which you are operating changes quite suddenly. A business concept is usually designed to meet users' needs under a certain set of environmental conditions, but if those conditions change, then the business concept will likely need to be adapted to account for that change. This is what happened amid the COVID-19 pandemic—many business concepts and ideas were suddenly no longer relevant as the pandemic took hold, and those entrepreneurs were forced to iterate aspects of their businesses.

What does iteration look like? What options do you have before you when you decide you need to iterate? In his book *The Lean Startup*, Eric Ries (2011) identified and described different types of pivots that founders might consider when they discover that their current business concept is not working as intended. These pivot types, as described by Ries, create a useful template to understand the iteration options that entrepreneurs might consider. In turn, the iteration options can be organized into three distinct categories: product-related iterations, customer-related iterations, and business model–related iterations.

Product-related iterations pertain to changes in the product or service offered by a venture. These may include the following:

- *Zoom-in iteration.* A zoom-in iteration occurs when a founder discovers that one feature (or a few features) of an initial product or service is (are) the most valuable for users, and the founder decides to zoom in to make that feature (or features) the whole product. In Chapter 3, I described how the founders of Instagram—Kevin Systrom and Mike Kreiger— had originally created a scrappy yet complex location-based check-in app called Burbn that allowed users to check in at specific locations, message other users to make plans for future meetups, earn points for hanging out with friends, and post pictures of their social activities. Although Burbn captured some early users, growth quickly stagnated, and the founders realized something needed to change. They examined how people were using their product and discovered most people were just using the app to share photos. They therefore iterated by zooming in on just the photo-sharing feature of the Burbn app, and Instagram was born.

- *Zoom-out iteration.* A zoom-out iteration entails expanding the feature set of an initial product or service, going from just a simple product or service to a more expansive suite of offerings in the product or service. This may happen systematically over time, or it may happen more dramatically in one fell swoop. An example of a systematic zoom-out pivot comes from the online "robo-advising" investment platform Wealthfront. They initially offered just one simple investment product, but over time, they iterated to add savings and cash account options, checking functionality, and credit facilities to provide a full suite of financial functionality to clients.
- *Technology shift.* A technology shift entails shifting the underlying technology at the core of a product. This could be because the initial technology does not work as intended or because a new technology has emerged that is more valuable for the product or service being developed. A famous example of a technology shift is Netflix, where Reed Hastings drastically iterated from focusing on DVDs delivered by mail to online streaming. Ultimately, he was still delivering home entertainment in the form of movies and TV shows to users, but he shifted to do it via a very different technology platform.

Customer-related iterations pertain to changes in the customers served and the means for connecting with those customers. These may include the following:

- *Customer segment shift.* A customer segment shift is simply changing the segment of customers being served. When Airbnb (mentioned in Chapter 1) was conceived, the founders focused on customers attending conferences, conventions, and events as their primary target market. They even used the Democratic National Convention as the focal point for launching the first iteration of their product because it drew attention to their event-based focus. However, they soon discovered that events were too sporadic to support the Airbnb model, and they shifted to focus on general travelers who were traveling primarily for leisure. This constituted a customer segment shift for the venture, and it paid off handsomely.

- *Customer need iteration.* A customer need iteration is a shift in a business's core proposition to focus on a different customer. In other words, the founder changes what the business does to focus on a different customer "job to be done." One of the most well-known customer need shifts was the creation of Twitter. Twitter was born out of another business called Odeo, which aimed to help users create and distribute podcasts before podcasts were even a thing. Odeo was not taking off as the three founders had hoped, so they started experimenting with different ideas, and the concept of sharing what you were doing or thinking with friends via a short text message was born. This was the creation of Twitter. It served a different customer need from that of creating and distributing podcasts, as Odeo had intended to do, but still had the distribution of information at its core.

- *Channel change.* A channel change is a shift in the channel that a venture uses to distribute and deliver its product or service to customers. Many ventures had to change their delivery channels amid the COVID-19 pandemic. Numerous entrepreneurs and business owners had to shift to an online channel as physical locations shut down. Personal trainers shifted from in-person classes at gyms to online training sessions, education institutions shifted from offering classes in physical classrooms to offering those same classes online, and restaurants had to shift to in-home food delivery channels to maintain demand for their products. A channel change may also come about as a founder discovers a more efficient and effective channel for delivering their product or service.

Business model–related iterations pertain to changes in the basic business model of a venture. A business model iteration may include the following:

- *Pricing pivot.* A pricing pivot is a significant shift in the price point for a particular product or service. In some cases, such a pivot may entail dropping the price or even making a product or service free. In other cases, it may entail increasing the price to increase profit margins or create a better balance between supply and demand. One of the things I discovered in a prior corporate training venture I founded was that a substantial upward price pivot resulted in greater demand for our products and services because customers appeared to associate higher quality and more desirability with a higher price.
- *Value capture change.* A value capture change is essentially a change in the mode, mechanism, or timing for collecting revenue from customers. It might entail shifting from a once-off transaction to a subscription model, as many software firms did as they transitioned to a software-as-a-service model. It might entail shifting from an advertising-based model to a paywall model or vice versa. It might entail moving from a pay-for-service revenue model to a retainer-based revenue model or from a commission-based model to a fixed-fee model. All of these reflect value capture changes for a venture. A successful value capture change was implemented by the fitness wearable firm Whoop, which developed a device that tracks heart rate variability, sleep, strain, and recovery and provides that data back to the user via a mobile app. When Whoop first launched, they sold the device for close to $500, but this was a big barrier for many people. Will Ahmed, the founder of Whoop, said

that he learned from studying Peloton, and based on Peloton's pricing structure, he shifted from a once-off transaction as a mechanism for value capture to a subscription model. With this iteration, sales took off. Customers found it much easier to sign up for a two-year contract at $30 per month ($720 total payment) compared to paying $500 upfront to purchase a Whoop strap.

- *Cost structure change.* A cost structure change is just what the label implies, making some change in the business to radically alter the cost structure. This can sometimes be done in conjunction with a pricing pivot (discussed previously), but it could also be done independently. This change may entail a shift from in-person coaching or therapy sessions to online sessions, thereby eliminating the need for an office or a consulting space and substantially reducing cost. Shifting to a remote work structure for employees could have a similar effect. It could also entail drastically increasing the cost base to offer customers a more premium or luxurious product or service.

These different types of iterations are not mutually exclusive. It is highly likely that one type of iteration may be coupled with other types of iteration. For example, a channel shift may be coupled with a technology shift if a firm pivots to an online channel and needs the underlying technology to support that, as was the case with Netflix when they shifted to a streaming model to deliver television and movie content. A pricing pivot and cost structure change are very often coupled together.

The different types of iteration options can be depicted on a matrix so that founders can easily see what options are at their disposal. This matrix breaks down the different iterations by category—product, customer, or business model—and highlights the specific types of innovations within each category, as depicted in Figure 6.1.

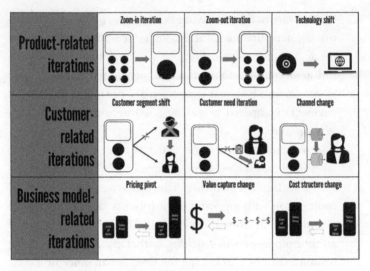

Figure 6.1 The iteration matrix.

Fully Embracing the Iteration Principle on Your Entrepreneurial Journey

So how do you know if you are fully embracing the iteration principle to make meaningful progress in your entrepreneurial endeavor? The key to doing this is to be constantly learning and willing to change what you are doing based on what you learn. Enacting the iteration principle builds on the insights and perspectives generated from enacting the other principles—especially the prototype and experimentation principles—but iteration entails acting on feedback received to change a product or service to more closely align with the needs of the market.

Fully embracing the iteration principle in the entrepreneurial journey entails the following:

- Learning from key stakeholders about what works and what does not work in your product and service

- Getting input and perspectives from mentors, other team members, or experienced founders to help you evaluate feedback and decide what needs to be iterated
- Asking yourself, *if this was my best friend's business and they received feedback on their business similar to the feedback I have just received, what would I advise them to do?*
- Making changes to your product or service based on feedback received from stakeholders (including feedback from customers, suppliers, investors, employees, etc.)
- Considering iterations and changes in three broad areas to find better product-market fit: (1) product-related iterations, (2) customer-related iterations, and (3) business model–related iterations
- Monitoring all iterations that are enacted to see if they generate business improvements

Ignoring or overlooking the iteration principle in the entrepreneurial journey entails the following:

- Ignoring feedback from stakeholders
- Blaming key stakeholders, such as customers, for not understanding your product or service when they don't use it as intended or when they ignore it
- Thinking you are smarter than your customers or other key stakeholders
- Becoming locked into the core idea of what your business should be and not being willing to change from that in the face of feedback
- Always thinking you know better than everyone else

The best entrepreneurs iterate. Almost no successful business does what the founder initially set out to do in the way they thought they would do it. Founders learn from their actions and change their businesses in response to what they learn.

PART II
THE ACTION PRINCIPLES

7

The Hustle Principle

In Chapter 1, I described how Sara Blakely cut the feet off her pantyhose to create a new style of undergarment that ultimately became
Spanx, the revolutionary women's shapewear. At the time, she was
27 years old and struggling to make a living selling fax machines
door to door. She had no business degree and less than $5,000 in
savings. With her footless pantyhose prototypes, she convinced a
hosiery manufacturer in North Carolina to produce a limited run
of commercial samples for her and, even then, only after the repre-
sentative from the manufacturer shared the idea of footless pantyhose with his wife and daughters. He could not see the value in
what Sara had created, but they could. They persuaded him to give
it a shot.

With commercial samples in hand, Sara started cold calling department stores. Now, getting a new product into a department
store is no easy feat; in fact, many who have tried will tell you it's
impossible. The challenge is even greater if the department store
is well known and high end. On the *How I Built This* podcast, Sara
described her efforts to get into Neiman Marcus as her first retail
account:

> I called them.... I just called them. I went in the Yellow Pages, and
> I looked at the Neiman Marcus number in Atlanta, and I said, "Hi,
> I'm Sara. I invented a product. Can I come and show it to you?"
> And the lady laughed and goes, "Ma'am, we have a buying office,
> and it's in Dallas." And I said, "Oh, what's their number?" So, she
> gave me their number and I started calling them, and I just kept
> calling and trying to get to the hosiery buyer. And I called for days

The Principles of Entrepreneurial Progress. Greg Fisher, Oxford University Press.
© Oxford University Press 2024. DOI: 10.1093/oso/9780197669815.003.0008

at different times, and she answered the phone, and I took my shot, and I said, "Hi, I am Sara Blakely, and I invented a product that is going to change the way your customers wear clothes. And if you give me a few minutes of your time I will fly to Dallas and show you." She said, "Well, if you are willing to fly here, I will give you 10 minutes of my time." And I said, "Great!" And I jumped on a plane, and I flew to Dallas. And I was in the meeting with her, and she was this beautiful woman, impeccably dressed. I'm in the Neiman Marcus headquarters. I have a Zip Lock bag from my kitchen with the prototype in it, a color copy of the packaging that I had created on a friend's computer, and my lucky red back-pack from college that all of my friends begged me not to bring.... In the middle of my meeting with her, I could tell I was losing her, and I just knew it was my one shot, so I said, "You know what, Diane, will you come with me to the bathroom?" And she just paused. She goes, "Excuse me?" I go, "I know, I know, it's a little weird. Will you just please come with me to the bathroom? I want to show you my own product before and after." And she said, "Okay." And she walked down the hall with me, and I went in the stall, and I had on my cream pants that were the reason I invented this without Spanx on, and then I went in the stall and put Spanx on and came out. And she looked at me, and she goes, "Wow! I get it! It's brilliant." And she says, "I am going to place an order and put it in seven stores and see how it goes." I couldn't believe it. I got in the car, and I was shaking (Blakely, 2017).

After this experience, Sara worried that Neiman Marcus would drop the product if sales weren't strong, so she called up everyone she knew and enlisted them to purchase Spanx off the shelf. She later mailed each of her friends a reimbursement check, bringing her total profits to zero but keeping perceived demand high.

Although unorthodox and clearly unsustainable, these urgent and deliberate problem-solving behaviors are not atypical for entrepreneurs in the earliest stages of their businesses as they seek to make progress with their new ventures. In many instances, such actions are necessary and the only means to facilitate progress.

In an interesting research project, from which the story above about Sara Blakley emanated, my colleagues and I transcribed and coded the interviews with successful entrepreneurs from 48 *How I Built This* podcast episodes, and we observed these types of behaviors time and time again.

We observed how Jerry Murrell, the founder of Five Guys restaurant, went to the parents of his sons' friends to raise capital for his first store. He described his experience as follows:

I can remember going in the bank, and they said, "You're gonna do what?" I said, "I don't represent just another hamburger place," and they just laughed at us. So, my sons said, "We got friends, and their parents got a little bit of money, and they know Five Guys is doing good. Maybe we'll ask them for a few thousand." So, we got some people that would be willing to give us money but not as investors—just loans. We did it a different way. We said, "Give us $5,000, [and] we'll give you a certain percentage of the gross [revenue]"—not ever the profit because there would be too many ways to cheat people that way. So, I said, "We'll give you a certain percentage of the gross [revenue]. We'll give you the money every single month, and anytime you want your money back you can have it," and everybody said, "Well that's stupid because if you have a blip, everybody's gonna come in and ask for the money back." But my method in my madness was also that I said to them, "Any time I want to pay you back, I can." I knew someday if this thing was successful, I was gonna get better financing. I could go back to these people and pay them back anytime I wanted (Murrell, 2019).

We were intrigued by Gary Erikson, the founder of Clif Bar & Company, who engaged in various grassroots marketing efforts. He recalled:

I did a couple things. One is I would go to bike races or I went to running events and just started passing out the bars. We did one advertisement in bicycle magazines and a few other magazines that was pretty hard-hitting against PowerBar. Was like, "Okay! There is a new kid on the block" kind of thing. The headline was, "It's your body, you decide. Do you want refined ingredients, or do you want whole ingredients?" and pictures of both ingredients. That caused us to be sued immediately! Our insurance picked up the tab, and we ended up settling with PowerBar. But it created this buzz in the bicycle industry where people said, "Hey! Have you heard of Clif Bar?" I don't know if you could pull that off now because there are hundreds of bars out there. But back then it was just us and them (Erikson, 2018).

We were fascinated by Sadie Lincoln, the founder of the exercise studio network Barre3, who described how when she moved to Portland, Oregon, she could not find an appealing exercise class, so she quickly began creating her own exercise experience centered around creative ballet routines. After a while, she invited friends to join her (at no cost), and the classes were so popular that she realized there was an opportunity for a group fitness studio focused on upbeat ballet routines. This helped her conceive of and create a thriving business. There are now more than 130 Barre3 studios across the United States, Canada, and the Philippines (Lincoln, 2018).

And we were captivated by Brian Scudamore, the founder of 1-800-GOT-JUNK, who said that one of his challenges was to find out where he could take other people's junk. "I just called up the city municipalities and said, 'Where do I take a load of junk if I've got some?' and they gave me the addresses of all the different places, and I quickly tried them all out. Some were closer than others; some were cheaper but farther away. I experimented quite a bit, but it was pretty easy stuff. I mean it really was a business of pick up someone's junk, see the smile on their face, take their stuff off to the dump or to be recycled, and repeat" (Scudamore, 2018).

In each case, the entrepreneur took clear action with a sense of *urgency*—they acted as though there was an impending deadline. And in each case, something spurred them to act to resolve an issue or seize an opportunity in an *unorthodox* way, beyond what you might learn in business school or see within a large established corporation.

We labeled this behavior "entrepreneurial hustle" and defined it as "an entrepreneur's urgent, unorthodox actions that are intended to be useful in addressing immediate challenges and opportunities under conditions of uncertainty" (Fisher et al., 2020: 1012). In this research paper, we identified how such urgent and unorthodox behaviors help entrepreneurs uncover new opportunities, learn more about what they are doing, forge unexpected relationships, access resources they would otherwise not have had, and establish their ventures as legitimate entities.

We concluded that hustle behavior is a necessary but not wholly sufficient ingredient for entrepreneurial success. Hustle needs to be combined with other principles of entrepreneurial progress to facilitate success, but without it, the chance of any entrepreneurial success is almost zero.

The Principle

Entrepreneurship is about action. It's about an individual or small team recognizing that they have the agency and ability to do something meaningful. To do that, however, they need to act, and often, they need to act in ways that are unorthodox and to do so with a sense of urgency. Acting in ways that are unorthodox means that entrepreneurs go beyond the obvious avenues to solve problems. They go "above and beyond" to embrace novel, creative, and often surprising solutions to challenges. This means they may engage in "guerilla" tactics, bricolage, bootstrapping, and/or resourceful actions that allow them to discover creative solutions. In so doing, they can circumvent traditional practices and processes that may impede or slow progress for someone trying to do things in more orthodox or conventional ways. They can also discover solutions and ways forward that are nonobvious and interesting and that can be carried out with the limited resources they have on hand. It's a means to make meaningful progress.

Beyond just acting with unorthodoxy, entrepreneurs who get things done often act with a sense of urgency. They push, they rush, and they make things happen more quickly than might seem reasonable. They do so because they recognize that they are the energy behind what they are doing; they can't rely on anyone else to generate that energy and make things happen. In larger, more established organizations, there are often routines and practices that can be employed to get things done, but in a newer venture, those routines and practices don't exist yet—getting things done depends on the energy of an entrepreneur. Moreover, in some sense, an entrepreneur is in a race against time. In a startup, an entrepreneur typically has a limited pool of resources, and the longer anything takes to get done, the more those resources will be eaten up before any significant progress is made. Acting with urgency allows for progress to be made in the limited time at hand.

The Hustle Principle:
Entrepreneurial progress entails *acting in urgent, unorthodox ways* to overcome challenges.

Engaging in hustle is valuable for several reasons. Entrepreneurship is a prolonged journey with many steps, obstacles, and setbacks. Entrepreneurial hustle can be a resourceful action for removing these obstacles, obtaining key resources, and addressing significant shortcomings. Entrepreneurial hustle can sometimes create a sense of momentum when things seem to have stalled; acting with urgency and unorthodoxy enables an entrepreneur to find a way through setbacks and challenges.

The research on entrepreneurial hustle suggests that it enables and supports many aspects of the entrepreneurial process. Hustle helps entrepreneurs create opportunities, overcome resource constraints, learn valuable information, establish legitimacy, and foster connections under conditions of uncertainty. Each of these things can be critical to making significant progress and keeping the momentum going in the entrepreneurial process. Next, I discuss how hustle can impact each of these aspects of entrepreneurship.

Hustle for opportunities. Acting urgently and in unorthodox ways to overcome challenges and seize opportunities, entrepreneurs are often able to spark new insights and perspectives that can lead to new products, processes, or the pursuit of new markets, thereby creating entrepreneurial opportunities that would not have existed without entrepreneurial hustle. For example, after Sadie Lincoln moved with her husband from San Francisco to Portland, Oregon, she struggled to find a workout option that suited her. To solve this, she began creating her own workout routine, which was a combination of ballet, yoga, and Pilates. Over time she invited others to join her, and because of urgently solving her own problem in an unorthodox way, she created a new type of workout that she called barre. This evolved into the workout studio Barre. Barre has now become a global phenomenon and Barre3 expanded to 130 studios worldwide by 2022.

Hustle for resources. Most entrepreneurs don't have all the resources they need to launch a new venture. Entrepreneurial hustle is a means to mitigate resource constraints. Many entrepreneurs can either convince others to provide some of the resources they need or find a way to utilize on-hand resources in novel, unorthodox ways to overcome obvious resource constraints. Entrepreneurial hustle also enables entrepreneurs to enroll supporters in what they are doing. In our initial research study on entrepreneurial hustle (Fisher et al., 2020), we used an experimental approach to assess whether entrepreneurial hustle has any impact on potential new venture stakeholders. The presence of entrepreneurial hustle in a description of an entrepreneur prompted people to perceive the entrepreneur as more trustworthy in their ability to manage uncertainty and caused these evaluators to be more likely to support the venture, thereby serving as a mechanism to overcome resource constraints.

Hustle for learning. Entrepreneurs often operate with new technologies and unfamiliar business models in unproven markets, all of which contribute to their uncertain environments. To mitigate uncertainty, entrepreneurs need to be open to learning and exploration. One of the most productive ways to learn about new technologies, models, and markets is to engage with them (Cope, 2005). Entrepreneurial hustle enables learning in an uncertain environment. By hustling, entrepreneurs can quickly try things out, get rapid feedback, and discover new insights and perspectives that are not readily available elsewhere. Hence, they can learn quickly and effectively about technologies, business models, and markets.

Hustle for legitimacy. Entrepreneurial ventures confront the liability of newness—meaning that because they are new, they are not well known, understood, or accepted and hence have a lesser chance of garnering acceptance and support and a greater chance of failing (Stinchcombe, 1965). In other words, they lack the legitimacy needed to make progress. Legitimacy is a social judgment of acceptance, appropriateness, and desirability (Suchman, 1995). Being perceived as legitimate enables new ventures to overcome the liability of newness and thus attract external approval and support. To mitigate their liability of newness, new ventures may seek to actively establish their legitimacy (Fisher et al., 2016). Entrepreneurs who engage in urgent, unorthodox actions often make their ventures appear bigger, older, and more professional than what they are, thereby engineering legitimacy for their ventures through their hustle.

Hustle for connections. Entrepreneurs depend heavily on links with others to support and validate their efforts. Creating and maintaining a network of relationships is a critical entrepreneurial activity. However, forging new relationships with other individuals or entities is not necessarily easy for entrepreneurs; their liabilities of newness and smallness make it difficult to establish meaningful connections. Yet, entrepreneurs who act quickly to find points of convergence and establish reasons and means to connect with others often create valuable connections that can have a significant impact on their ventures' trajectories.

It is clear from this list that hustle has a wide-reaching impact on entrepreneurship. An entrepreneur who is not willing to do things that are somewhat unorthodox with a sense of urgency is likely to lose out to an entrepreneur who is willing to do so. So how does one do this?

The Practice and the Tool

Some people may think that hustle—acting in urgent, unorthodox ways to overcome challenges—is something that some people just do naturally, while others are not inclined to hustle and may therefore struggle to make entrepreneurial progress. However, my colleagues and I have found through research that there are a few things that can make a big difference when it comes to an entrepreneur's likelihood of hustling.

First, just being aware of the concept of hustle and its impact on entrepreneurial progress can be important for entrepreneurs. Understanding the concept can provide insights into how entrepreneurs behave, which can in turn impact that individual's own behavior in the entrepreneurial journey. Understanding the hustle concept can open an individual's eyes to what it means to be entrepreneurial and thereby help them act in more entrepreneurial ways as they embark on the entrepreneurial journey.

Second, in my research I have found that giving oneself permission to hustle can make a big difference when it comes to making progress and pushing new ideas forward. Just recognizing what hustle is and then taking note that it can be a useful way to act in the entrepreneurial process can not only facilitate increased levels of hustle behavior but also, in so doing, enable entrepreneurs to overcome institutional and bureaucratic barriers that might otherwise significantly impede entrepreneurial progress (Fisher, Stevenson, and Burnell, 2020). So, if possible, consciously give yourself and your team "permission to hustle."

To help entrepreneurs think about what hustle might look like, my colleagues and I developed a crude hustle equation (see Figure 7.1), which accounts for (1) the short-term outcome that one desires in the entrepreneurial process, (2) the action that will be required to achieve that outcome, (3) how that action might be carried out with urgency, and (4) how it can be accomplished in an unorthodox way. This equation won't tell you exactly what you need to do or how you need to do it, but it will help you think through how you can incorporate more hustle behavior into what you are doing so that you can leverage its benefits in your entrepreneurial journey.

Fully Embracing the Hustle Principle on Your Entrepreneurial Journey

To fully embrace the hustle principle on your entrepreneurial journey, it is useful to really appreciate and understand what hustle means. Start by listening to stories of how other entrepreneurs have had to hustle in their effort to create a new venture. The *How I Built This* podcast is a great source of such stories. My colleagues and I developed the concept of entrepreneurial hustle by analyzing the stories shared on this podcast, and in turn, the podcast can be a

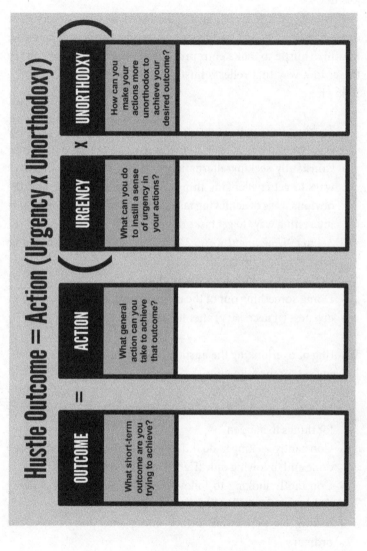

Figure 7.1 Hustle elements.

source of inspiration, insight, and perspective when it comes to developing and implementing hustle behavior in the entrepreneurial journey.

However, it is not enough to just listen to what others have done. Hustle is based on how an entrepreneur acts. Therefore, to utilize hustle to make entrepreneurial progress, it is necessary to act in a way that reflects hustle behavior. This will entail the following:

- Tackling tasks with a sense of urgency and operating as if time is scarce and it is critical to get things done as soon as possible
- Constantly seeking alternative, creative, out-of-the-ordinary ways to get challenging things done and looking beyond the obvious ways of achieving tasks to uncover less obvious, more interesting ways to get tasks done
- Asking *"How might we . . . ?"* regularly to uncover alternative ways to get things done
- Constantly looking for workarounds
- Doing something out of the ordinary and then asking for forgiveness (if necessary) after it is done

Ignoring or overlooking the hustle principle in the entrepreneurial journey entails the following:

- Tackling tasks in a slow methodical way or, worse still, waiting for things to happen
- Constantly seeking to do things the way they have always been done and following only tried-and-tested procedures
- Constantly looking to follow the rules and only ever doing things that fit within predefined policies
- Asking for permission before doing something out of the ordinary

The best entrepreneurs hustle. Engaging in hustle does not ensure entrepreneurial success, but if you are not willing to hustle at least a little, it is highly likely that you won't manage to surmount the challenges you will confront as an entrepreneur, and you will most likely fail. As such, hustle is a necessary but not a stand-alone behavior for entrepreneurial success.

8

The Story Principle

When doing things that are novel, it is often very challenging to describe to others what you are doing or why you should be the one pursuing your idea. Most people just don't get it. But the one way you can help them "get it" is through stories. Stories are the most natural and effective way for people to process new information, and as such, *storytelling is an entrepreneurial superpower*. Whether you are telling a story about the origin of your idea, the challenges that you have overcome, or the path you are taking into the future, stories help you clarify what you are doing and connect in meaningful ways with others who might be able to support you in your efforts. Consider this example from Kindra Hall's (2019) book *Stories That Stick*:

> It was season five of Shark Tank when a mother stood before the toothy investors. She was there to pitch her line of baby moccasins, and this mom knew her stuff. She answered every tough biz question the Sharks threw her way. Margins, customer acquisition cost. They asked the question; she had the answer. And yet the waters looked murky. None of the Sharks seemed particularly interested in investing. That is, until the Utah mother found the opportunity to tell her founder story. It wasn't necessarily about the footwear but rather about the other product she was selling: herself. She told them what it took to get the company started. She had the idea, yes, but ideas take money, and money was something she didn't have much of. To raise enough funds to get her first products made, she spent an entire summer breaking the glass out of aluminum window frames. Grueling work, sweaty

The Principles of Entrepreneurial Progress. Greg Fisher, Oxford University Press.
© Oxford University Press 2024. DOI: 10.1093/oso/9780197669815.003.0009

work, bloody work. Once the frames were cleared, she brought the aluminum to a scrap yard where they gave her a total of $200. She used that $200 to buy fabric for her first few moccasins. It wasn't until the Sharks heard her story that the water in the tank turned from lukewarm to a total feeding frenzy (97–98).

The Airbnb founders, whom I mentioned in Chapter 1 because of their efforts to build a business to solve their rent-deficit problems, also benefited from the power of storytelling at a pivotal moment in their startup journey.

The first year of building Airbnb was tough—*very tough*—for Brian Chesky and Joe Gebbia. The founders had been through many rough patches in their efforts to bring the business to life. They had maxed out multiple credit cards and endured a few false starts. Airbed and Breakfast was a novel idea, and it had huge potential, right? What started as a surefire money-maker was beginning to cast shadows of doubt. They were uncertain whether they could make it, but their one big opportunity was to try and land a spot in Y Combinator—Silicon Valley's most respected venture accelerator program. This opportunity was like the golden ticket to the chocolate factory. Acceptance to Y Combinator would provide them some cash and, more importantly, access to top-notch mentors to help them figure out their growth path. After months of preparation, they were ready for the pitch.

However, following the initial pitch, the hum of the overhead lights suddenly became the loudest thing in the room as all Y Combinator partners looked confused. Y Combinator cofounder Paul Graham was especially perplexed. Gebbia described the interaction as follows:

"You mean people actually use this?" Paul asked. And we go, "Yeah." And he goes, "Well, that's weird." It's not a great way to start an interview of any kind. It kind of went downhill from there. We're walking out of the room, and I'm thinking like,

"This is our last chance effort, and it didn't go so well." And that's when I remembered that I had brought a box of Obama O's to give to him [Paul Graham] as a gift. So, I go running back into the room, I whip out the box, I hand it to him and said, "Hi Paul, we got this for you." He goes, "Oh, where did you buy this?" I go, "Well, we made it." He goes, "What do you mean you made it?" And I told him the story in 60 seconds, and he goes, "Wait, so you guys funded your company based on selling breakfast cereals?" And he immediately turned around and put the box of cereal on the shelf behind his desk. On the ride home, we get a phone call from Paul Graham to inform us that he'd like to offer us a spot in the Y Combinator program. And we later found out that the reason we got in wasn't because of our idea; it was because through the breakfast cereal we had proven to him that we had hustle. . . . If we could figure out how to sell breakfast cereal for $40 per box, we could figure out how to make our website work (Gebbia, 2017).

Joe Gebbia managed to tell the right story at the right time, and it made all the difference in the trajectory of Airbnb. The stories you tell don't need to be extended tales with complex plotlines. However, sharing who you are, what you are doing, why you are doing it, what challenges you have overcome, and what trajectory you are taking into the future in the context of a story will help you bring so many more people along on your journey, including investors, employees, suppliers, customers, journalists, and just general supporters.

When Slack founder Stewart Butterfield was asked what he learned when pivoting his venture from developing his online game Glitch to the organizational platform Slack, this was his response: "If there was one piece of advice I wish I could phone back and give to myself [it would be] just concentrate on that storytelling part, on the convincing people. Because if you can't do that, it doesn't matter how good the product is, it doesn't matter how good the idea was for the market, or what happens in the external factors, if you don't have the people believing" (Butterfield, n.d).

The Principle

Entrepreneurship is about creating a future that does not exist yet, but doing do requires entrepreneurs to not only make sense of what they are doing but also to share what they are doing with others to garner support and input. As humans, we have evolved to be most receptive and responsive to information conveyed in the form of a story. Therefore, if we want to get a better sense of what we are doing and get others to buy into it, we need to be able to transform our ideas about where we have come from and where we are going into a story.

The Story Principle:
Entrepreneurial progress entails *crafting a story* to describe what you are doing.

Stories—as we know—include a beginning, middle, and end with transitions that link these phases through characters, purpose, and plot (Mills and John 2020, 2023). As the protagonist of their stories, entrepreneurs can construct meaningful accounts of events to not only make sense of what they are doing for themselves and their teams (Lounsbury and Glynn, 2001) but also create meaning where none yet exists for external stakeholders who may support their endeavors (Lockwood and Soublière, 2022). In so doing, founders engage in *strategic entrepreneurial storytelling*—they incorporate various entrepreneurial narrative types into a coherent story (Fisher, Neubert, and Burnell, 2021).

The different entrepreneurial narrative types that entrepreneurs may invoke include identity narratives (Navis and Glynn, 2011), narratives specifying opportunities to be pursued (Garud and

Guiliani, 2013), narratives projecting future states (Garud, Schildt, and Lant, 2014), narratives claiming attributions for failure (Mantere et al., 2013), narratives describing a pivot or change (McDonald and Gao, 2019), and narratives detailing an entrepreneur's resourcefulness (Fisher, Neubert, and Burnell, 2021). These different narrative types each serve a particular purpose, and entrepreneurs often use them alongside one another to forge a richer, more nuanced entrepreneurial story (Burnell, Neubert, and Fisher, 2023).

Narrative #1: The identity narrative. Identity narratives represent claims about "who we are," "what we do," and "why that matters" (Navis and Glynn, 2011). Such a narrative describes how an entrepreneur, venture, and market all fit together (Navis and Glynn, 2011; Zott and Amit, 2008) and may include an origin story that describes a founder and the historical roots of a venture (Mills and John, 2020, 2023). An identity narrative must include a coherent story connecting an entrepreneur's background and experiences to the focal venture opportunity and the broader context. A disconnect between these elements can introduce doubt in audiences about a venture's plausibility.

Narrative #2: The opportunity narrative. Opportunity narratives portray connections between problems in the world and what can be done to fix those problems. A good opportunity narrative conveys a sense that an entrepreneur has discovered a big problem or was alert to an unmet market need (Kirzner, 1999). Such a narrative describes how the entrepreneur investigated and understood a significant problem; the narrative conveys the entrepreneur as a hero discovering the holy grail of value. Then, in response to such a discovery, the entrepreneur must convey what solution they have created and how they created such a solution to potentially solve the problem they discovered. As such, opportunity narratives usually include elements of both discovering problems and then creating solutions.

Narrative #3: The projective narrative. Entrepreneurial journeys often entail a projected vision of the future, and entrepreneurs can make the future appear more comprehensible and plausible with a projective narrative. A projective narrative sets the plot for an entrepreneur's broader story by constructing different social and material elements into a compelling chronological account that invites stakeholders to imagine future venture possibilities (Garud, Schildt, and Lant, 2014). In so doing, entrepreneurs can make sense of the future for themselves and for new venture audiences, and they can generate excitement about what they are doing by plotting a plausible account of the best possible future that could unfold. To do so, their narratives often offer specific examples or illustrations about the future and include concrete steps to get to that future state.

Narrative #4: The failure narrative. The entrepreneurial journey often entails obstacles, setbacks, and challenges. These obstacles introduce conflict into the broader entrepreneurial story that prevents an entrepreneur from achieving their objective. To account for this conflict, entrepreneurs often construct failure narratives. An entrepreneurial failure narrative is an account of a particular failure event that has occurred during the entrepreneurial journey (Shepherd et al., 2016). It allows for an entrepreneur to acknowledge failure, recover internally from the failure event, and reconcile damaged relationships with external venture audiences. Constructing effective failure narratives entails *acknowledging causes*, including any personal role in the failure, while also conveying learning by embedding lessons from the failure within the story.

Narrative #5: The pivot narrative. Pivot narratives convey how entrepreneurs change their strategies or aspects of their business models (Grimes, 2018; Kirtley and O'Mahony, 2020; Shepherd et al., 2023). Entrepreneurs must craft pivot narratives to "reorient their strategies while minimizing penalties from their key audiences" (McDonald and Gao, 2019: 1314). Penalties from key audiences may arise when those audiences don't understand a pivot or when they are scared by the change implied by a pivot. In constructing pivot narratives, entrepreneurs should justify change by providing reasons and rationale for the proposed change based on new evidence, and it helps to connect change to prior aspirations. By seeking empathy for their ventures' current challenges, entrepreneurs can craft compelling justifications for change that do not alienate their audiences. In so doing, they should also reaffirm their commitment to the problems they are solving and the value propositions of their ventures. This includes providing content within their stories that shows they are committed to solving the problems they identified and developing excellent products despite struggles or obstacles.

Narrative #6: The resourcefulness narrative. The entrepreneurial journey contains elements of overcoming challenges in pursuit of one's goals. Resourcefulness narratives are "accounts of past or ongoing entrepreneurial actions, whereby an entrepreneur is presented as using, assembling, or deploying resources in creative ways in order to overcome an impediment" (Fisher, Neubert, and Burnell, 2021, 6). Two elements are important for an effective resourcefulness narrative. First, a resourcefulness narrative must portray an entrepreneur as using, assembling, or deploying resources in creative or unorthodox ways. That is, the entrepreneur must have been or is currently undertaking an activity considered novel or unusual without regard to resources under their control. Second, a good resourcefulness narrative must include an impediment that an entrepreneur is trying to overcome. This impediment could be lack of financial capital or simply a challenge or some sort of structural obstacle the entrepreneur must face to move their venture forward.

But entrepreneurial stories are about more than just the narrative. Research highlights that the signals and symbols that entrepreneurs evoke in and around their ventures and what they do in terms of communicating their story effectively matter almost as much as the story itself (Bafera and Kleinert, 2023; Clarke, 2011; Zott and Huy, 2007). Signals can help enhance a story—for example, signaling that you have built a prototype and incorporating your prototype into your entrepreneurial narrative can show that you are action oriented and willing to build your ideas, rather than just talking about them. Also, signaling the experience and education of the founding team and their investment in and commitment to a venture can make an entrepreneurial story more credible and impactful for venture stakeholders, as can signaling that there are others interested in what you are doing and possibly even willing to partner with you. Symbols also matter, and they can be very subtle. Dressing in a certain way to highlight something important about what you are doing, invoking the symbols used by other successful entrepreneurs, or even meeting stakeholders in a particular location to tell your story can make the story seem more credible and impactful.

So, the underlying message here is that entrepreneurial stories really matter when it comes to convincing others that what you are doing is important, but stories are not told in a vacuum, and the signal and symbols used to enhance and support the stories you tell are as important as the stories themselves.

The Practice

In considering these six narrative types more holistically (see Figure 8.1 adapted from Burnell, Neubert, and Fisher, 2023), it is evident that each narrative is just one aspect of a broader entrepreneurial story and each narrative type can be supported or enhanced with key signals and symbols. A broader entrepreneurial story often begins with identity, opportunity, and projective narratives to make sense of the focal entrepreneur, emerging opportunity, and projected future. These elements represent the typical narrative

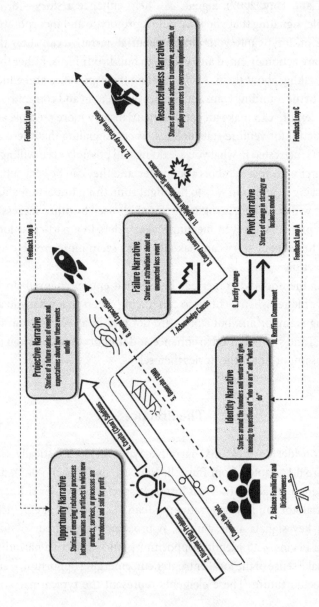

Figure 8.1 Narrative elements of entrepreneurial stories.

elements of a protagonist, the pursuit of the protagonist, and the foreshadowing of events, respectively (Fiol, 2002).

Failure, pivot, and resourcefulness narratives then become more salient as the entrepreneur progresses through their journey and takes actions to move their venture forward. At later points in the entrepreneurial journey, the entrepreneur must reach into their past to explain and justify their actions. They narrate what challenges they encountered (i.e., failure narrative), how they changed after confronting these challenges (i.e., pivot narrative), and what they did to creatively overcome impediments to achieve their goals (i.e., resourcefulness narrative).

Beyond narrative combinations and sequences, entrepreneurs may also consider the narrative audience. For pitching situations with investors, identity narratives, opportunity narratives, projective narratives, and resourcefulness narratives appear most relevant. Traditional investors use identity narratives and resourcefulness narratives to make sense of the "jockeys" (i.e., the entrepreneurs), whereas opportunity and projective narratives help investors make sense of the "horses" (i.e., the opportunities). One could think of identity and resourcefulness narratives as developing a story's main character, the opportunity narrative as developing the purpose, and the projective narrative as developing the plot. Without these ingredients, the story may fall flat with investors. By contrast, while failure narratives can help investors make sense of failure events after investment, these narratives may create doubt in investors' minds by indicating a record of problems.

The audience for a new venture might go beyond investors and may include people like customers; partners; or internal venture stakeholders, such as the founding team or early employees. Regarding internal venture stakeholders, pivot and failure narratives become particularly important because an entrepreneur may need to process a failure and reaffirm commitment after an adverse event. Overall, the key takeaway is that as an entrepreneur, you need to understand that your audience matters when constructing an entrepreneurial story. Entrepreneurs should construct narratives with a particular audience in mind and tailor these narratives to address that specific audience's unique expectations and preferences.

The Tool

To begin to craft a story, it is useful to think about and capture ideas pertaining to the seven Cs of a story: context, characters, challenge, conflict, course of action, climax, and conclusion. The template in Figure 8.2 can serve as a prompt to identify and then connect these different elements.

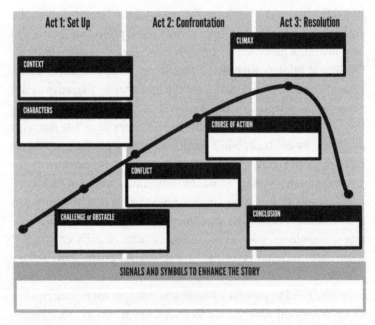

Figure 8.2 A story template: the seven Cs.

Context. The context accounts for the details of the situation surrounding an entrepreneurial endeavor. It entails specifying the type of setting and circumstances in which the entrepreneur starts their story. In storytelling settings, context plays a huge role in connecting the storyteller and their ideas to the reader. To make a story more powerful, entrepreneurs should aim to make the context for their story vivid, real, and detailed.

Characters. Characters are the people involved in an entrepreneurial endeavor. They may include the users who experience the problem that the venture seeks to solve. They may also include the entrepreneur and the venture team. Story scripts have a range of different characters, and as a founder constructs an entrepreneurial story, they will need to decide which of these are relevant:

- Protagonist. The protagonist is the main character in the story. This person is the focus of the story, the person the storyteller wants readers to invest in and care about. In the context of an entrepreneurial story, this could be an individual who suffers because of the problem the new venture seeks to address, or it could be the entrepreneur themselves.
- Antagonist. This is the villain, the character who opposes and undermines the protagonist. It could be the person creating the problem the new venture seeks to address, or it could be the people behind the competitor organization the new venture seeks to displace.
- Sidekick. The sidekick is a character who supports the protagonist. In the case of an entrepreneurial story, this could be a mentor, investor, or other type of venture supporter (assuming the entrepreneur is the protagonist), or it could be someone else who suffers because of the problem the new venture seeks to address.

Challenge. Challenge is the central issue or problem that at least one of the story characters confronts. It is a difficulty that needs to be overcome. In the context of entrepreneurship, this could be the central problem the venture is addressing, or it could be the difficulty the entrepreneur is having/has had in setting up the venture.

Conflict. Conflict arises over time because of the challenge. It accounts for the difficulties the central character has had in their efforts to address and overcome the challenge or obstacle they confront.

Course of action. The course of action is the steps/path the central character takes to begin to navigate beyond the conflict and overcome the challenge. In the context of an entrepreneurial story, it may pertain to the steps the entrepreneur takes to solve a complex problem or overcome a major venture impediment.

Climax. The climax is what happens as a result of the course of action. It is a breakthrough or a resolution to the critical issue, a good outcome. In the context of an entrepreneurial story, it may include achieving a major venture milestone or having overcome a significant impediment.

Conclusion. The conclusion is where the story ends. Many times, it links back to the original context but with some major change having occurred. In the context of an entrepreneurial story, the conclusion likely involves an overarching resolution by solving a problem.

All these elements are reflected in the story template in Figure 8.2. This story template breaks down these elements across three phases or acts in story terms: Act 1 is the setup, Act 2 is the confrontation, and Act 3 is the resolution. This template also signals the emotional intensity associated with the different story elements. Emotional intensity is somewhat low at the beginning when the context and characters are introduced, and it increases as the story progresses with a challenge, conflict, course of action, and climax until it drops off with the story's conclusion.

The template also provides space to consider the signals and symbols that may enhance a story. Here an entrepreneur can consider what they might signal to others as they tell their story—things such as education, investment, commitment, support from others, and progress can all be useful signals that can come through in a story narrative or alongside a story narrative. You can also think about what symbols can be invoked to enhance your story—clothing, colors, meeting contexts, and other things can be symbols that may enhance the credibility and legitimacy of the story you tell.

Fully Embracing the Story Principle on Your Entrepreneurial Journey

To fully embrace the story principle, it is important and useful to practice storytelling. Stories don't always resonate the first time you tell them, but the more you experiment with and iterate your stories, the more likely they are to evolve into something that resonates with others. Therefore, keep experimenting with crafting and telling stories, and as you do, make note of how different audiences react to various versions of the stories you tell. Keep what works and discard what doesn't work, and in so doing, you will become increasingly better and will develop a valuable story archive.

Listening to the stories of other entrepreneurs can also help you identify what makes an entrepreneurial story resonate. So, similar to the advice given in the hustle principle chapter (Chapter 7), it is useful to listen to entrepreneurial stories told on the *How I Built This* podcast to get a sense of effective (and less effective) entrepreneurial storytelling.

Fully embracing the story principle in the entrepreneurial journey entails the following:

- Understanding the elements of a story and identifying how they relate to your entrepreneurial journey
- Experimenting with different entrepreneurial story structures to see what resonates with key audiences

- Adjusting your story as you attempt to appeal to different audiences—trying to understand the needs and perspectives of different audiences and relating your story to their unique needs and preferences
- Taking note whenever a version of your story seems to hit home so that you can build on that version of your story the next time you need to share what you are doing with others
- Seeking and seizing opportunities to get your story out there—seeking out pitch competitions, seizing opportunities to be a case study, working with journalists to create media articles, participating in podcasts, accepting invitations to talk at events or to university students, etc.

Ignoring or overlooking the story principle in the entrepreneurial journey entails the following:

- Conveying what you are doing with statistics and figures but never linking them together into a coherent story
- Not taking the time to understand the elements of a story and/ or ignoring how they relate to entrepreneurship
- Ignoring how audiences react to what you say when sharing details about your venture
- Failing to adapt your description of your venture to the needs and desires of different audiences
- Failing to look for opportunities to share details about your venture story

Many effective entrepreneurs are good storytellers, and telling stories creates momentum in their entrepreneurial journeys. Storytelling is a skill that can be learned, and it gets refined through practice. Therefore, if you want to leverage stories as a means to move your venture forward and get support for what you are doing, you need to become cognizant of what it takes to be a good storyteller and practice storytelling as part of your role as an entrepreneur.

PART III
THE RESOURCING PRINCIPLES

9

The Control Principle

How would you go about establishing the truck and trailer rental company U-Haul from scratch? Today, U-Haul has thousands of trucks and trailers at hundreds of locations across the United States, and the value of renting a U-Haul truck or trailer is that you can rent it at one location and drop it off at another location, thereby allowing customers to haul stuff easily and efficiently across the country. But how might one get this company started? This is a thought experiment that Professor Saras Sarasvathy from the University of Virginia famously poses with the MBA students in her class. She described this thought experiment in her influential article titled "Causation and Effectuation: Toward a Theoretical Shift from Economic Inevitability to Entrepreneurial Contingency" (Sarasvathy, 2001).

Here are some of the details of U-Haul's founding used by Sarasvathy and provided by Silver (1985: 387–390):

> Like many other successful ventures, the concept for U-Haul was provoked by need. After World War II the population of the United States became more mobile and migratory. There existed an obvious widespread need for do-it-yourself moving equipment on a one-way, nationwide basis. It was the visionary approach of U-Haul that recognized this need, acted upon it, and literally created an industry.
>
> With $5,000, L. S. Shoen, his wife Anna Mary Carty Shoen and their young child moved to the Carty ranch in Ridgefield, Washington. There, with the help of the Carty family, the Shoens built the first U-Haul trailers in the fall of 1945, using the ranch's

The Principles of Entrepreneurial Progress. Greg Fisher, Oxford University Press.
© Oxford University Press 2024. DOI: 10.1093/oso/9780197669815.003.0010

automobile garage (and milk house) as the first manufacturing plant for the budding U-Haul Co.

By the end of 1949, it was possible to rent a trailer one-way from city-to-city throughout most of the United States.

Sarasvathy (2001: 248) noted that the historical facts of U-Haul's founding are that in four years and with just $5,000 and access to an automobile garage, the Shoen family created a "nationwide firm with a complicated production function, thousands of stakeholders, and what was essentially 100 percent market share in the newly created do-it-yourself moving industry." This transformation is riddled with a complicated set of decisions: How many moving trucks and trailers should be bought and transformed (or made)? How many locations are needed? How many employees should be hired (one per location or more)? What will it all cost, and where will the necessary capital come from? How should the service be priced?

According to Sarasvathy, in class discussions using the creation of U-Haul as a case study, "students typically come to one of two conclusions:

- This project is not financially viable—the resource requirements are very large (estimates range between $20 million and $50 million in current dollars) and overwhelm any attempt to price the service viably, OR
- This project is not viable psychologically—even if it were financially viable and potentially profitable, the initial resources required would be so large as to raise the question of why anybody with control over $20 to $50 million would want to invest it in this relatively mundane but risky project consisting of buying trucks and renting locations across the country" (Sarasvathy, 2001: 248).

However, as Sarasvathy explained, U-Haul was created with an almost instantaneous national presence for a very small financial outlay. Instead of trying to raise the money to buy a large number of trucks or trying to start the company with very few locations, the Shoen family focused on the resources that were under their control—stretching their $5,000 in capital, leveraging the rudimentary manufacturing facility on the ranch, and forging powerful relationships with others who could help them bring their vision to life. Overall, they focused on how they could best leverage those resources to move their idea forward. Sarasvathy broke down some of the Shoen family's key decisions as follows:

- They began by establishing an identity. Their first few trailers were painted bright orange, and the name "U-Haul Co." was established. The trailers were emblazoned with the sales message "U-Haul Co., Rental Trailers, $2.00 Per Day" on their sides and back, which meant they were always advertising, whether they were being hauled on the road or parked on display.
- They convinced friends, family members, and customers (who then convinced others close to them and so on) to individually make downpayments on trucks and then lend the company the trucks for use.
- They contracted with service station outlets (including national chains) to merchandise trailer rentals, eliminating the need to buy space in cities across the country and to recruit employees to man the spaces.
- They offered early customers discounts on their trailer rentals for establishing U-Haul rental agents at their destinations and established a commission structure for dealers.

Thus, with hardly any employees and a very small outlay of funds, U-Haul came into being. The Shoen family did this by focusing on maximizing the resources under their control; they focused on what they had and did not dwell on what might be needed. This is how they made progress despite the mountain of challenges they confronted.

A more recent story illustrating the importance of focusing on what you have under your control—your means—as opposed to dreaming about how much money you might make is the founding story of Calendly, the online scheduling tool founded by Babatope "Tope" Awotona. Growing up in Lagos, Nigeria, Tope's entrepreneurial interests took hold as he observed and felt the effects of the wealth disparity in the region. Knowing he never wanted to struggle or cause his family to struggle from financial insecurity, he looked to entrepreneurship as a way out and up.

Tope moved to the United States in his teen years and began working in various sales positions, including for IBM after graduating from the University of Georgia. His days were spent working on client accounts, and his nights and weekends were dedicated to finding the entrepreneurial venture that would springboard him into a future as a founder. His first idea was to build a dating site after reading an article about these sites' recent success. Tope invested in a few domains and bought a few books on coding but quickly abandoned the idea after realizing he didn't have the skills, resources, or broader means necessary to get it off the ground (Khan, 2019).

Tope then connected with a broker who told him there was a great opportunity to sell data projectors online. "And so, this guy told me that there was an opportunity to start an e-commerce business, specifically an e-commerce business selling projectors. So, he had done some kind of analysis and figured out that if I built an e-commerce website for projectors, I could create the opportunity to rank really highly for some heavily searched terms. And that's how I got into selling projectors," said Tope (Awotona, 2020). He ran the website for a while, but he wasn't seeing a lot of business; he didn't care much about the product; and it wasn't leveraging any unique skills, perspectives, or personal resources. This wasn't the money-making endeavor he was passionate about. He admitted he didn't know a lot about the problem he was solving for his customers.

Sensing the fit wasn't there and facing poor margins on his sales, he began looking for a new opportunity.

His third idea was a website that sold home and garden equipment, which had better margins, but he eventually discovered he wasn't any more enthusiastic about grills than he was about projectors.

Tope thought back to why he wanted to become an entrepreneur and realized he was so focused on making money by whatever means possible that he forgot about his own passions and interests, as well as the unique perspectives and skills he could bring to a business. He decided that the only way to have any kind of longevity in business was to solve a problem he truly cared about and, in so doing, to use the unique attributes he possessed. He also felt that in his attempts to find the right fit, he was just "burning money," although he had learned valuable lessons along the way. Tope decided to take a sabbatical from his mad dash to entrepreneurial success and focus on problems that he was connected to (Albert-Deitch, 2019).

The idea for Calendly came to him a short while later. Tope recalled, "I was trying to maybe coordinate a meeting across maybe three different companies with about 10 to 20 people, I forget exactly how many. And it was just so painful. And so, the problem that I had was I was just trying to, you know, corral all those people" (Awotona, 2020). Tope started to search for a solution that would allow him to coordinate schedules and wasn't finding exactly what he was looking for. The problem was clear, and he saw the solution in his mind's eye. At the same time, though, he remembered what it felt like to fail, and for months, he looked for reasons not to pursue the venture. However, as time went on, Tope realized he was uniquely positioned to take on this venture. His prior experience in sales and the lessons he had learned in starting his prior website ventures put him in the unique position of really understanding the problem and having the means to develop something to solve it.

Tope used his savings to launch Calendly in 2013. He did not squander time and energy trying to convince investors to fund his idea prior to having a product. He used what he had on hand to oversee the development of the first version of the Calendly software. Recalling that time, he said that although he had some doubts, he embraced the philosophy that "now is the time to do this. Nothing is guaranteed. You can try to wait for the perfect moment, the perfect idea, or the perfect development sequence, or you can start with this place and with what you can do and expand from there" (Awotona, 2020). He cobbled together what he had to make his idea happen, which entailed tapping into his savings, borrowing some money from a lending club, and doing almost all the product conceptualization and requirement specification himself even though he did not have experience developing software. "I created my own detailed list of requirements and detailed flows that needed to happen, that needed to be built. And also, my own sequence of how the work needed to be done" (Awotona, 2020). Taking control of these elements gave him a huge advantage when he did start working with developers. Not only did his focus on what he had on hand to solve a personal problem reduce the cash outlay for development, but also it gave him an intimate understanding of the product and its nuances so he could properly oversee its development.

Calendly was created as a cloud-based service that allows groups of people to quickly manage open spaces in their respective calendars to find time for appointments or meetings. The software then books the time in users' personal or work calendars, filling it seamlessly and decreasing the back-and-forth tedium of trying to find open time (Lunden, 2021). Eventually, Tope was able to convince outside investors that the business had promise, but only after he made significant progress by focusing intently on leveraging and maximizing the resources under his control.

Today, in 2022, Calendly has 10 million monthly users, up significantly after the pandemic forced more people home, who found themselves needing new ways to connect (Sawers, 2021). Following a $350 million round of fundraising, the company's estimated valuation rests at $3 billion (Latimore, 2021). As for the future? Tope said he's eyeing the meeting lifecycle and looking for ways to build on the competitive advantage Calendly has carved out for itself. In May 2021, Calendly announced a new suite of features for enterprise management, suggesting the company is exploring more business-to-business applications for additional growth.

The Principle

Often entrepreneurs focus almost all their energy and attention on what they need from the outside to start a business. They make lists of what they don't have and try formulating plans to get those items. For many years, writing a business plan was seen as a critical entrepreneurial activity as it was thought to be the ticket to convincing investors or partners to provide financial capital or other resources to a venture. While I was a contributor to *Entrepreneur Magazine* between 2007 and 2013, the most requested information was about writing a business plan because founders viewed it as a means to get resources, and they viewed getting resources as the most important thing they could do in starting their businesses.

This is very problematic. There are two major interrelated problems with this mindset and approach.

The first problem is that focusing intently on what you don't have puts you squarely in a scarcity mindset. You continually feel like you don't have enough of what you need and therefore have the sense that you cannot act. The natural response to being in this scarcity mindset is to wait to take any substantive action until you get the resources you need; it creates a "wait and see" perspective and orientates you away from acting to make progress to establish and build a venture. Entrepreneurial progress is about action, but if you have a scarcity mindset and a "wait and see" perspective, you are less likely to take the action needed to actually make progress.

The second problem is that this mindset and approach make you very dependent on others; you cede control of what you are doing to outsiders who have the resources you need. Entrepreneurship is by its nature a very uncertain path, but by depending on others for resources, you make it even more uncertain because you hand over control of your endeavor to those who can supply resources.

To overcome these problems, expert entrepreneurs shift away from focusing on what they need to focusing much more intently on what they have under their control. Saras Sarasvathy's research (2001, 2009) highlights that expert entrepreneurs consider how what they have under their control can be used to achieve their goals and aspirations. Such entrepreneurs intuitively focus on (1) who they are, (2) what they know, (3) what they own, and (4) who they know when figuring out how to move forward to create or exploit an entrepreneurial opportunity. They build off what is immediately under their control so they can act quickly and definitively rather than depending on additional resources from others to take action. Sometimes, this means shifting one's immediate aspiration to something that is smaller, more accessible, and more doable, but doing so allows momentum to be created, and that smaller aspiration is often the steppingstone needed to achieve the bigger, more elaborate goal.

This can be encapsulated in the control principle, as follows:

The Control Principle:

Entrepreneurial progress entails *maximizing the resources under your control.*

In my experience, applying this principle empowers and energizes entrepreneurs. It gives them a sense of agency over what they are doing and allows them to navigate a path forward that is less dependent on others. While their ventures will still likely get funding and resources from outsiders, maximizing the use of resources under one's control early in the entrepreneurial process allows entrepreneurs to create momentum and build something that will then make it much easier to get external resources at a later stage.

The Practice and the Tool

Applying the control principle entails first taking account of the resources under your control and then following that up by using those resources to engage in entrepreneurial action.

To take account of the resources under your control, you can consider different categories of resources, including (1) who you are, (2) what you know, (3) what you own, and (4) who you know.

Who you are. Who you are includes your traits, tastes, abilities, and attributes—the things that are unique about you as a person. This entails doing a careful stock-take of what a founder brings to a venture in terms of their personal attributes.

What you know. What you know includes the things you have knowledge and insight about. These resources often stem from your education, training, skills, experiences, and capabilities. This accounts for insights, perspectives, and knowledge that a founder has developed over time.

What you own. What you own accounts for the physical resources and other assets that you (and your founding team) have under your immediate control. These resources could include computer equipment, a phone, a vehicle, financial resources, and any other kinds of assets that may be of value for a new venture.

Who you know. Who you know refers to your connections and relationships—the people within your social networks. These resources could be work connections, but they could also be broader, more wide-reaching connections, such as friends, acquaintances, and other people you may have access to. To take account of your connections, reflect on the people you and members of your founding team know. List all relationships under different relationship categories, such as friends and family, prior colleagues, acquaintances, etc.

The means you control under your venture are the sum of the resources that come from these four categories. After assessing the four categories, you can then ask, "What can I create with what I have under my control?" The notion is that you don't need to depend on others to act using these resources. You don't need to pitch, wait, and wonder whether others will buy in and support you. You can just act. And acting is what moves a venture forward.

The tool in Figure 9.1 can help with brainstorming the resources in these different categories. This tool prompts you as an entrepreneur to think about your means—who you are, what you know, what you own, and who you know—such that you can then leverage and use these resources in novel ways to build your business.

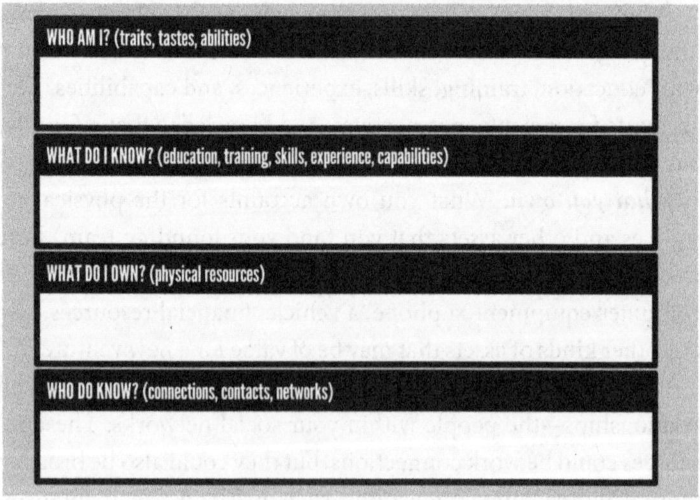

WHO AM I? (traits, tastes, abilities)

WHAT DO I KNOW? (education, training, skills, experience, capabilities)

WHAT DO I OWN? (physical resources)

WHO DO KNOW? (connections, contacts, networks)

Figure 9.1 A means-based analysis.

Having filled out the worksheet in Figure 9.1, it is important to step back and ask: "How might I use these resources under my control to move my venture forward?" Recognizing the resources under your control and questioning what can and should be done with those resources (including your traits, tastes, abilities, education, training, experience, capabilities, physical and intellectual resources, and connections, networks, and contacts) is a powerful way for figuring out how to take action to move your venture forward.

Fully Embracing the Control Principle on Your Entrepreneurial Journey

To fully embrace the control principle as you pursue an entrepreneurial endeavor, it is critical to focus strongly on the resources under your control as a basis for deciding what you are going to do in the early stages of launching a venture. Taking account of these resources in terms of who you are, what you know, what you own, and who you know creates a foundation from which you can decide what your initial, doable, and immediately actionable first steps in venture creation will be. It is from these first few steps, dictated by the resources under your control, that you can then begin to create momentum and progress in developing your business.

Fully embracing the control principle in the entrepreneurial journey entails the following:

- Taking stock of the resources at your disposal as you start on the entrepreneurial journey
- Using the resources at your disposal as a basis for deciding what initial actions you will take on your entrepreneurial journey
- Creatively combining different combinations of resources under your control—including who you are, what you know,

what you own, and who you know—in novel ways so as to create some value and test ideas early in your entrepreneurial journey

- Using resources in ways that are different from their intended purpose to make early progress in the venture development process
- Making progress on a venture using the resources under your control so you have something to show to resource providers when you ask them for funding or other types of support

Ignoring or overlooking the control principle in the entrepreneurial journey entails the following:

- Operating with the expectation that unless you can get investors to invest in what you are doing, you are not going to pursue it
- Seeking everything you need to get a venture started from external stakeholders
- Ignoring or overlooking who you are, what you know, what you own, or who you know as you launch a venture
- Using available resources only in the ways they were intended to be used and not being willing to get creative in your use of resources as you start a venture

10

The Affordable Loss Principle

Almost 20 years ago, when I decided to leave my job at Deloitte and launch my own venture in the learning and development space, I was terrified. I was scared that I would end up losing tons of money; I was paralyzed by the uncertainty of starting something new and stepping out into the unknown; and I had many sleepless nights, toiling in my mind with possible paths and contingencies that would dictate what might happen. Up to that point, I had been working for about five years, and I felt like I had managed to build up a buffer of personal capital, but if I lost all of that on trying to launch a new venture, I would be disappointed and inevitably regret my decision. I really wanted to avoid that anticipated regret. For many weeks, I struggled to move forward and make definitive decisions because I feared what would happen if I failed. Struggling to move forward, failing to make decisions, and operating from a place of fear is no way to start a business—it was perpetuating the problem.

A mentor then said to me that I should clearly specify for myself what I am willing to lose on this endeavor and that I should even take that amount of cash and set it aside in a separate account as capital that I am willing to invest (and lose) in starting the business. He told me that this shouldn't be an amount that would cripple me financially if I lost it and that I should try to let go of any emotional attachment that I might have to that capital. I needed to shift my perspective from seeing that as *my* capital to seeing it as the *business's* capital.

I did this. I took half of my personal savings and handed it over to the business. I became comfortable with the idea that if I lost

The Principles of Entrepreneurial Progress. Greg Fisher, Oxford University Press.
© Oxford University Press 2024. DOI: 10.1093/oso/9780197669815.003.0011

that capital, I would still be fine personally. That was what I could afford to lose, and it was what I needed to invest to give the business a reasonable chance of success. This shift in perspective was transformative for me and my mindset in launching the venture. I was no longer paralyzed by uncertainty and riddled with fear. Instead, I was freed up to make decisions and take action to move the business forward. If those decisions were wrong and I lost the capital, I knew that I would still be okay.

A few years later, after experiencing this transformation, I discovered that this concept had been described in the academic literature. It was called the "affordable loss principle," and it was part of the theory of effectuation put forth by Saras Sarasvathy of the University of Virginia (Sarasvathy, 2001). Sarasvathy, whom I mentioned in the previous chapter, had studied the decision-making protocols of expert entrepreneurs and realized that most applied the idea of affordable loss when making decisions amid uncertainty. The experts would only invest what they were willing to lose. She identified that they would minimize the risk of a project by only investing what they could afford not to have. After examining expert entrepreneurs applying this principle, she noted that they predetermine how much loss is affordable and focus on experimenting with strategies to succeed with the given means at their disposal.

After learning about the affordable loss principle, I started to notice that successful entrepreneurs apply this mode of thinking and some of them do so with other resource categories besides just financial capital. For example, back in 2017, Adena Hefets decided to take on the challenge of making housing more affordable and accessible to lower-income Americans. This was something Adena cared about deeply as she had been exposed to these difficulties personally: "My parents were immigrants and came here without any money" (Hefets, 2021). Adena noted a shrinking lack in options for homeownership and realized that this had knock-on effects for many low-income families. Why wasn't the industry adapting as the environment changed to help more people begin to build equity through their homes? she wondered.

Together with Brian Ma and Nick Clark, the trio created Divvy Homes in 2017 to address this issue. Divvy lets an individual pick out a home, and then Divvy buys it, acting as the title holder and allowing the individual to rent the home with lower payments for three years while still building equity in the home that they are renting (Nguyen, 2020). Ultimately, when the individual is ready to buy the home, they can do so at a prespecified price and use the equity they have built up over their time as a renter as part of the downpayment. This is a difficult business model to master. It necessitates getting various stakeholders and business model elements to work together effectively, and when Adena set out to solve this problem, she was not sure she could make it work. When asked on the *ExecuTalks* podcast if she feared it might fail, this was her response:

> Oh my gosh, yes, all the time. I remember saying this is a really interesting problem. I think I have a solution that can help people. Let me just try to put it out there in the world, and I remember I time-boxed it in my head, not like actually time-boxed it, but mentally, I said, "I am going to give this six months. I want to see what I can do in six months." And at the end of six months, I was like, "Oh I feel like we have a couple customers. People are actually really excited about this. Let's give it another year. I want to see myself make this much profit in the next year." And so, then we did that, and it was like, "OK, let's keep going," and it slowly built on itself, and so today, it is something that I will hopefully do for the rest of my life (Hefets, 2021).

Divvy has now helped thousands of people get into new homes across 16 different markets, and the business is valued at more than $2 billion (Azevedo, 2021). To get to that point, Adena applied the concept of affordable loss to *time* instead of to financial capital.

She had to figure out and specify how much time she was going to dedicate to making progress toward solving this problem and then stopped second-guessing herself while she focused on forward progress. Time-boxing her commitment gave her the freedom and mental space to focus on the issues at hand.

The Principle

Embarking on an entrepreneurial path is risky, and if an individual or team is constantly worried about what they might lose and what is at stake as they attempt to develop a new venture, they are likely to constantly second-guess themselves. They are more likely to be paralyzed by uncertainty and fear of failure. To overcome this paralysis, it is valuable to figure out what you can afford to lose in the process of starting a venture. This may include financial capital that can be invested in the venture without too many negative ramifications, or it may account for the time that you or your team are willing to invest without second-guessing whether you are doing the right thing.

Specifying upfront what you are willing to invest (and hence lose) in starting a venture and setting that aside cognitively and/or physically so you know what you have on hand to get the venture started can be incredibly freeing. It allows you to focus on the most important issues to make progress rather than constantly being paralyzed by fear of failure and wondering whether what you are doing makes sense.

Accordingly, affordable loss becomes an important criterion on which to base startup decisions. Entrepreneurial experiments that would cost more than the focal entrepreneur can afford to lose are rejected in favor of more affordable experiments. Thus, in applying the affordable loss principle, entrepreneurs should view new venture activities as experiments in which losses are contained. Additional resources are added only if justified by the results of those experiments (Chandler et al., 2011). This approach allows venture teams to make substantial, meaningful progress in moving their ideas forward without bankrupting themselves or their ventures.

The Affordable Loss Principle:
Entrepreneurial progress stems from *specifying the resources you can afford to lose* in pursuing your idea.

Sarasvathy and Dew (2006) explained that by applying the affordable loss principle, entrepreneurs try to estimate the downside and examine what they are willing to lose in order to start a venture. They then use the very process of building a venture to bring other stakeholders on board and creatively leverage the resources on hand to make progress without utilizing more resources than they can afford to lose. Estimating what is affordable does not depend on the venture but varies from entrepreneur to entrepreneur and even across an entrepreneur's life stages and circumstances. By allowing estimates of affordable loss to drive their decisions, founders don't need to depend on trying to predict complex, ambiguous outcomes under uncertain circumstances. Focusing on affordable loss pushes entrepreneurs to worry much less about expected returns and more on what they can do with what they have on hand. Focusing on expected returns is much more complex than affordable loss. To calculate expected returns, an entrepreneur needs to estimate future sales and possible risks that constitute the cost of capital and then raise enough money to make the venture happen. To calculate affordable loss, all an entrepreneur needs to know is their current resource position and a psychological estimate of their commitment in terms of the worst-case scenario.

The affordable loss principle also dictates that founders find creative ways to bring their ideas to market using the resources and connections they can assemble, thereby further extending and enhancing the control principle (Fisher, 2012). The application of the principle forces an entrepreneur to look for the cheapest alternatives and come up with creative ways of doing things at little or no cost to themselves.

The Practice and the Tool

Applying the affordable loss principle is about reasoning from your life situation, your current commitments, your aspirations, and your risk propensity. Applying this principle can be conceptualized as an iterative multistep process.

The first step is to ask how much you think you need to launch your venture. This may entail figuring out how much you think you need for different aspects of venture creation, product development, and initial launch and scaling. Getting creative about different ways to bring your idea to market using the means available to you and reducing the means you need to launch your venture is key to making this number seem reasonable.

The second step is to ask what you are willing and able to lose to start your business. This means thinking through your available resources and your risk preferences. What can you afford to lose? It can be useful to mentally account for resources in different categories—time, savings, home equity, credit cards, loans, etc. You may not want to utilize all of these resource categories, but the resources you are willing to access (and lose) are the sum of what you have on hand; they represent your immediate means. This resource amount is what you can and want to spend on starting your venture.

The third step is to assess whether the resources you have and are willing to lose are enough to cover what you need to launch your venture (from step one). In most cases, you won't have enough, and this is where you need to get creative:

- What else can you do to reduce the resources needed to get started?
- What else could you do to get additional resources from external stakeholders?
- How else can you leverage what you have—skills, resources, experience, connections, etc.—in innovative ways to do things that will help you get your venture started with less?

Once you are able to create some sort of match between what you have access to and can afford to lose (your means) and what you think it will take you to get started, then you can decide how you will allocate your means to start your business. The tool in Figure 10.1 can help you make this allocation.

The key takeaway of this principle is this: managing risk like a seasoned entrepreneur means making decisions based on acceptable downside risk rather than on guesses about upside potential. Reasoning through the decision to get started using the affordable

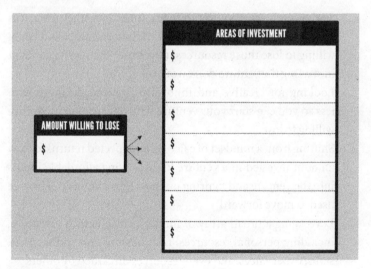

Figure 10.1 Affordable loss analysis.

loss principle reduces the perceived barriers to starting your business and helps you see how to begin while still managing your risk. Starting a business doesn't have to be determined by whether the upside is big enough; rather, you must decide whether the downside is tolerable.

Fully Embracing the Affordable Loss Principle on Your Entrepreneurial Journey

The affordable loss principle entails clearly establishing what you are willing to give up in launching your venture and separating that out cognitively and/or physically so you can use it for your business. Doing so will enable you to avoid constantly having to mix personal and business choices as you spend resources to experiment with your business ideas.

Fully embracing the affordable loss principle in the entrepreneurial journey entails the following:

- Setting aside an amount of money, time, and other resources that you are willing to dedicate to starting a venture and being willing to lose those resources if the experiments you conduct in starting the venture don't work out
- Looking for creative and innovative ways to do more with less so you can start your venture with only resources you are willing to lose
- Shifting from a mindset of calculating expected returns for any amount invested in a venture to calculating affordable inputs into the venture and figuring out how those inputs can best be used to move forward
- Leveraging a broad array of inputs to help launch a venture, including personal resources, relationships and connections, skills, experiences, and even resources discarded by others

Ignoring or overlooking the affordable loss principle in the entre-preneurial journey entails the following:

- Only focusing on what you think you need to start a business without considering what you can actually put into the business
- Using sophisticated return on investment and net present value calculations to justify investing resources in a venture
- Mixing your personal finances and resources with your business's finances and resources
- Never establishing any clear boundaries around the time and money you intend to invest in your venture

Managing resources is one of the trickiest and most challenging aspects of launching a new venture. As an entrepreneur, you undoubtedly won't have all the resources you need, but to attract resources from others, you will need to make progress with the resources you have on hand. Applying the affordable loss principle is one of the most productive ways to effectively utilize and maximize the resources you have on hand.

PART IV
THE BIG PICTURE PRINCIPLES

11
The Trajectory Principle

I could not work out why my ideas were not resonating with the audience. It was frustrating and embarrassing. I was back in South Africa to share insights, perspectives, and ideas about entrepreneurship and building new businesses, but it felt like I was not providing any value. I was told the audience was filled with entrepreneurs and people with entrepreneurial intentions, but from what I could tell, most of them were confused and overwhelmed. I hate feeling like I am not connecting with my audience, so at the first break, I chatted with a few of them to try to assess what the problem was. After a few minutes of conversing, it struck me: I was talking about a different version of entrepreneurship from what they were doing day to day. I was referring to examples like Airbnb, Instagram, and Calendly, and I was talking about growth, disruption, innovation, and differentiation, but their central issues were more about day-to-day cash management, registering a company, and finding transport to be able to deliver their goods and services. In essence, we were talking a different language. It was at this time that I started to think carefully about different types of entrepreneurial ventures and why it is important to understand which category you fall into. After researching dozens of startups and speaking with hundreds of founders, I could distill the types of entrepreneurs into four distinct categories.

Some people launch a venture as a means of economic survival. For them, entrepreneurship is a necessity. This happens in instances where other forms of employment are not readily available. In South Africa, the youth unemployment rate is around 40%, so for individuals with only a limited education and no specialist skills, starting their own business may be the only viable option for them to make a living. In this instance, entrepreneurship is a means to stave off extreme poverty. These individuals may be viewed as *necessity entrepreneurs* because they are launching a venture out of necessity to make a living. However, not everyone launches a venture under these circumstances.

Other entrepreneurs have other professional options available to them. They could likely find a reasonable job and may even leave a good career to start a new business. For these people, entrepreneurship is a means to become their own "boss" and to liberate themselves from the control and expectations of others. In essence, they decide to be an entrepreneur as a lifestyle choice. Choosing an entrepreneurial path may allow them to live in a certain location, have greater control over their time, and/or make more money than they would make in full-time employment. These types of entrepreneurs typically create a business that grows in revenue to a certain point and then levels off. At this point, these entrepreneurs can sustain the lifestyle they desire so they keep operating their businesses to support that lifestyle. Such individuals can be called *lifestyle entrepreneurs.*

The third group of individuals are the people who are driven by the opportunity to scale a business. These individuals tend to have quite high levels of ambition for their ventures and seek to grow them as much as they can. Such entrepreneurs display a competitive orientation toward business, and they may open multiple locations or diversify distribution channels and/or product lines to foster new lines of revenue growth for their endeavors. These individuals may be viewed as *growth entrepreneurs* because they seek to continually grow what they started.

The final group of entrepreneurs are those who strive to create a new industry or have ambitions to completely disrupt the industry in which they are operating. They often introduce novel products or services that are substantially different from those that currently exist, and/or they introduce unique business models into a market category that may change the way business is done in that category. This type of entrepreneur can be labeled a *revolutionary entrepreneur* (Bhide, 2000).

The four different trajectories can be depicted on a graph where the x-axis represents revenue and the y-axis represents time. See Figure 11.1.

The nuances of fitting into one of these four broad categories are important from an entrepreneurial action standpoint and from an entrepreneurial team alignment standpoint (Morris and Kuratko, 2020). The actions to be successful as a necessity, lifestyle, growth, or revolutionary entrepreneur are unique from one another. If, for example, a lifestyle entrepreneur tries to employ some of the aggressive tactics and risk-taking strategies employed by a revolutionary entrepreneur, they are likely to do things that are inappropriate for their context and are more likely to fail.

One of the case studies that I often teach in my entrepreneurship class is that of the founding of Zipcar (Hart, Roberts, and Stevens, 2003). Zipcar was set up to offer hourly car rentals in urban and suburban locations. It was designed to be a replacement for car ownership in areas where it is expensive to own a car. It offered a strong value proposition, and the founder duo Robin Chase and

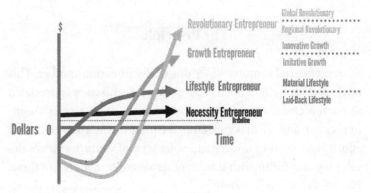

Figure 11.1 Different types of venture trajectories.

Anjie Danielson were very effective in getting the concept off the ground in 2002.

However, one of the nuances of the case is that different venture stakeholders appeared to see the venture in different lights. Robin Chase appeared to treat it as more of a growth venture, wanting to scale the business but not with the same aggression and speed as that of a revolutionary venture. Anjie Danielson treated it more as a lifestyle business in that she never left her full-time job to help run the company and was only partially committed to it even after they got funding. The investors wanted it to be a revolutionary venture, and they pushed hard for very aggressive growth. In fact, they eventually replaced Robin Chase as CEO so they could put someone in place that aligned more strongly with their revolutionary vision for the company.

These different perspectives across different venture stakeholders made it difficult for the team to figure out its path forward. I would argue that Zipcar would have had an easier time making progress in its early days of development and growth if all the venture stakeholders had been aligned in their vision for the desired trajectory of the business. By not identifying the right growth strategy, uncomfortable conflicts and departures from the management team resulted.

The Principle

Entrepreneurial ventures differ drastically from one another. This might sound obvious, but it is not always recognized or appreciated in startup circles. To increase your chances of success as an entrepreneur and to make meaningful progress in your venturing efforts, you need to understand what type of venture you are developing and distinguish it from other ventures that are out there. Having a clear understanding of the type of venture you are developing will have major ramifications for creating alignment in your venture team and for taking action to move your venture in the direction you intend for it to go.

One way to distinguish between different ventures is based on the intended trajectories of those ventures. At a very broad level, there are four venture types based on their different trajectories: the necessity venture, the lifestyle venture, the growth venture, and the revolutionary venture. Table 11.1 distinguishes between these different venture types.

These different trajectories can also be depicted in a figure, as reflected in Figure 11.1 with revenue in dollars on the x-axis and time on the y-axis. Here, you can see that the *necessity trajectory* starts just above the "breadline" and remains there as the entrepreneur operates. On this trajectory, a venture might grow slightly but not much. The entrepreneur operates the business day to day, just trying to make enough income to keep going and take a little bit out to enable survival.

The *lifestyle trajectory* highlights that the entrepreneur may need to borrow some capital or get a small outside investment to get started, after which they will start earning income. The aim is to then grow that income to a certain point, after which their revenue will plateau as they make enough income to sustain their desired lifestyle from one year to the next. Within this trajectory, it is possible to distinguish between those entrepreneurs who are striving for a laidback lifestyle, where income, material rewards, and financial success are less important than other lifestyle aspects, and those striving for a material lifestyle, where more time, effort, and energy are needed to generate more income and greater financial rewards.

The *growth trajectory* entails investing more in the business upfront, likely in the form of outside investment, to create a platform for growth and then looking for growth opportunities as the business matures. Within this trajectory, the entrepreneur can seek growth from imitation (doing activities or selling products similar

Table 11.1 Different Venture Types Based on Their Trajectories

	Necessity Venture	Lifestyle Venture	Growth Venture	Revolutionary Venture
Primary Aim	Develop and manage a venture to make enough income to survive	Develop and manage a venture that allows one to lead a desired lifestyle (based on location, autonomy, and income level)	Develop and manage a venture that continues to grow and scale	Develop a venture that disrupts and revolutionizes an industry or a market
Primary Motivation	Economic survival	Autonomy and lifestyle choices	Growth and competitiveness	Radical disruption and change
Investment	Very low	Low	Moderate	High
Risk	Limited	Limited	Moderate	High
Timeframe	Very short term (day to day or week to week)	Short term (month to month or year to year)	Medium term (3- to 5-year cycles)	Long term (5 to 10 years or longer)
Successful Outcome	Cash to eat and survival	Replacement of a typical salary with entrepreneurial income	Large competitive business and continued growth	Industry or market disruption and changing the face of an industry or market

to others) or innovation (engaging in activities or selling products that are different from others in valuable ways).

Finally, the *revolutionary trajectory* most likely requires the greatest upfront investment but will then grow at the most rapid pace if successful. Within this trajectory, the entrepreneur may seek to revolutionize things on a regional scale by focusing on a constrained and specific market or on a global scale with ambitions to operate across national borders. While there is a chance of business failure on all the trajectories, this chance is likely greatest for a venture pursuing the revolutionary trajectory because of the risks, difficulty, and uncertainty associated with trying to disrupt a market or an industry.

These different trajectories are depicted in Figure 11.1.

These trajectories matter for an entrepreneur because each has implications for how they will think about their venture and for the actions they take to make progress. If an entrepreneur is unclear about their trajectory, they are likely to find it much more challenging to figure out what action is appropriate to make progress. They risk taking steps that are at odds with one another, and they are likely to feel much less clear about what direction they should take. Understanding that they are pursuing a necessity, lifestyle, growth, or revolutionary trajectory provides a founder with guardrails and perspectives that allow them to make valuable choices and tradeoffs as they move forward.

The Trajectory Principle:
Entrepreneurial progress stems from *identifying a desired trajectory* and acting in accordance with it.

The Practice and the Tool

Applying the trajectory principle in practice requires you, as a founder, to practice self-awareness—you need to be honest with yourself about why you are doing what you are doing and what you want to get out of it. This awareness requires properly examining your motivation for starting a venture: are you most motivated by necessity and survival; by living a particular lifestyle;

by competitiveness and growth; or by the possibility of disrupting, creating, or revolutionizing an industry or market?

Your honest assessment of this question will put you and your venture on a specific trajectory and thereby create a specific vision for what you are doing. On a necessity or lifestyle trajectory, the vision for a venture is more modest, and the level of risk and uncertainty associated with that trajectory is somewhat mitigated. On a growth or revolutionary trajectory, a venture's vision is more grandiose, and the level of risk and uncertainty is also likely to be higher.

My experience of sharing insights about different venture trajectories with founders is that once they understand that the different trajectories exist and appreciate some of the nuanced differences between the different trajectories, they find it easy to identify which trajectory they need to be on with the venture they are creating.

This awareness can give an entrepreneur permission to do things that other entrepreneurs on different venture trajectories may see as unnecessary or outside their scope of activity. Examples of the more typical day-to-day activities and entrepreneurial actions associated with each venture trajectory can be found in Table 11.2.

Fully Embracing the Trajectory Principle on Your Entrepreneurial Journey

The trajectory principle entails knowing what kind of venture you are creating. This knowing is based on your motivation for starting the venture and on your goals and ambitions for what you hope to achieve through the venture.

Fully embracing the trajectory principle in the entrepreneurial journey entails the following:

- Carefully examining why you are starting a venture

Table 11.2 Entrepreneurial Actions and Activities Associated with the Different Types of Venture Trajectories

	Necessity Venture	Lifestyle Venture	Growth Venture	Revolutionary Venture
Entrepreneurial Actions and Activities	• Manage cash day to day • Focus on immediate sales and service • Pivot quickly to new opportunities • Work toward individual economic sustainability and stability	• Manage cashflow month to month • Balance debt levels with income generation • Incorporate lifestyle factors into business decisions • Work toward a longer-term lifestyle vision	• Focus on growth opportunities • Be willing to take on calculated risk to grow the business • Work toward a sizable business • Partner with equity investors to fund the business	• Work toward a big vision of doing things differently • Be willing to take on big risks to scale the business and disrupt the market • Partner with aggressive equity investors (e.g., venture capitalists) to fund the business

- Setting clear goals and ambitions for what you hope your business will become
- Realistically assessing how your venture will fit with other aspects of your life
- Understanding that different types of ventures necessitate different levels of investment and risk
- Aligning your day-to-day entrepreneurial actions and activities with your desired venture trajectory

Ignoring or overlooking the trajectory principle in the entrepreneurial journey entails the following:

- Believing that all entrepreneurial advice applies in all contexts

- Overlooking your individual desires, attributes, and ambitions in starting a business
- Looking for a one-size-fits-all approach to starting a business

Figuring out what trajectory you are on in your venture is not that tough, but remembering to align your day-to-day choices, actions, and activities with that trajectory can be. It is often tempting to do things that just don't align with your venture trajectory, but doing so could be detrimental to what you are doing. Aligning with your trajectory is the best way to ensure you achieve the outcomes you desire.

12

The Integration Principle

"To create the Tour de France of mountain biking." (G. Fisher, personal communication, September 18, 2011.) That was the stated aim of Kevin Vermaak when he set out to create a new multiday mountain bike race in South Africa in 2003. On the surface, the idea feels straightforward and achievable—until you learn that at the time, mountain biking hadn't been fully embraced by the mainstream, and Kevin worked in information technology in London.

"I was destined to be an entrepreneur and work for myself," Kevin said. "I lived my life up until that point with an assumption, rather than a dream, to work for myself" (Fisher and Goldman, 2012: 2). Key to his success, Kevin loved outdoor sporting events and would often travel to take part in them. Though he was born in South Africa, he used London as a homebase to go on several global hiking and biking expeditions to the Himalayas, South America, and New Zealand. On one of his trips abroad in Costa Rica, he competed in the La Ruta bike race, a three-day mountain bike race that takes competitors along the path of the Spanish conquerors of 1560 as they explored Costa Rica from the Pacific Coast to the Caribbean.

"La Ruta was a fairly small niche race, and it was expensive," recalled Kevin. He wondered if he could create a longer, larger, and more ambitious mountain bike race in his homeland of South Africa, something that would appeal to riders across the globe and generate valuable media attention. He was excited by the idea, recalling "a feeling of relief when I finally had an idea for which it was worth resigning and making a full commitment" (Fisher and

The Principles of Entrepreneurial Progress. Greg Fisher, Oxford University Press.
© Oxford University Press 2024. DOI: 10.1093/oso/9780197669815.003.0013

Goldman, 2012: 2). He began mapping out his idea and called the event the *Cape Epic*.

While South Africa offered quite a few world-class events in road cycling and running, most of these events had been set up and run as "not for profit" organizations. They depended on volunteers and often generated money for charity. However, Kevin wanted to create a business. To do this, he needed to think about the business model he wanted to employ and the sustainability of his event from day one. Therefore, he carefully considered and conceptualized how all the different components of his mountain bike race would fit together into a sustainable model.

He identified and defined his target customers as mountain bike professionals and high-level amateurs from across the globe. He specified how he would reach and maintain relationships with those riders via the internet and the event. He thought carefully about price points and other revenue streams (e.g., sponsorships and merchandise sales) for this business. He carefully assessed what infrastructure would be required to put on the event and what capabilities he would need to develop or acquire to deliver the event in a sustainable way year after year. Where possible, he forged partnerships to fill in key gaps, and he carefully assessed and monitored the costs of doing all this while mapping a path to profitability for his event. In short, Kevin was deliberate and structured not only in identifying the activities needed to ensure the race would be a successful business but also in setting up those activities so they would support and reinforce each other. In other words, he carefully integrated different elements of the business into a systematic and self-reinforcing business model.

It was this integrated business model that created the foundation for the growth and continued flourishing of the event for 20 years and counting. Kevin's clear understanding and careful management of each of the business model components and his insistence that those components not only support but also amplify one another allowed him to scale the event and make it a world-class spectacle without ever taking on outside investors. In 2016, he sold the event to the Ironman Corporation for an undisclosed large sum, and at the time, he was still the sole owner of the event.

Being deliberate about building a sustainable, self-reinforcing business model has also paid off for four MBA students from the Wharton School of the University of Pennsylvania. In 2010, they connected in their MBA program and had the idea to create a new kind of eyeglass company. At the time, the industry was dominated by one massive player—Luxottica—which was able to continually push up prices because of its industry domination. The impetus for the business came from a lost pair of glasses while one of the students was traveling the world.

David Gilboa, one of the four students, recalled, "I came back to the US. I was a full-time student, and I had to buy two things: a new phone [and] a new pair of glasses. And the iPhone 3G had just come out. I went to the Apple store and spent $200 on this magical device that did things that I couldn't have imagined were possible even a few years earlier. And meanwhile, I was going to have to pay several times that for a new pair of glasses. It's technology that's been around for 800 years, and it just didn't make sense to me as a consumer" (Handley, 2020).

The "vision" for the company was to adopt a direct-to-consumer model and sell glasses online. Before the MBA program, Neil Blumenthal, another of the four students, worked for VisionSpring, a nonprofit that helped provide affordable eyewear to developing countries. While there, Neil was able to see the production lines for the glasses intended for the developed and developing world and decided the former were unnecessarily marked up.

"We realized that there was kind of nothing in the cost of materials or nothing in the manufacturing process that justified these high prices. And so, that just really got us passionate, and [we] started talking about [how] this world doesn't make sense and [how] we should be able to create . . . a different model," David said (Gilboa and Blumenthal, 2018).

After presenting their idea at an MBA pitch competition, students Neil Blumenthal, Andrew Hunt, David Gilboa, and Jeffrey Raider were told that the direct-to-consumer model was impossible for the eyewear industry. Wharton professor Adam Grant remembers saying, "My first reaction was, 'That's ridiculous. You can't buy glasses over the internet. You have to go get your eyes tested, and then you have to try them on. This is not going to work'" (Handley, 2020).

The growing pile of constructive criticism forced the founders to think very carefully about their business model and prompted them to evaluate each aspect of the business carefully and deliberately. This led to several self-reinforcing business model innovations, including a carefully integrated supply chain, a simple and easy-to-navigate website, a clear low-cost price point, and what would become the company's most iconic offering—letting customers try on five pairs of glasses at home for free before buying any. The idea blew people's minds and prompted a *GQ* writer to pen an article about their fledging startup, calling it "the Netflix of eyewear." Their waitlist quickly grew to 20,000 people, and they hit their first-year sales target in just three weeks.

Warby Parker launched and grew with its innovative direct-to-consumer model, and after a few years, the company expanded from operating purely online to opening Warby Parker stores. Now, the company has 130 stores and 2,000 staff members, and it launched its contact lens line Scout in 2019.

Founders Andrew and Jeffrey went on to other adventures, but Neil and David stayed on as co-CEOs. The company went public in 2021, with the stock price soaring 30% on the first day of trading. The influx of investment is sure to tease out new improvements for what is already a highly disruptive and successful business. All this would not have been possible if the four founders had not carefully evaluated the existing business model in the eyewear industry and decided to reinvent each component of that business model in an effective way. As they did this, the founders ensured that each of their "new" business components fit with and reinforced one another in a mutually beneficial way. It was this innovative reinvention of the business model that allowed the founders to disrupt the eyewear industry in such a significant way.

The Principle

A business is a complex system. It has many components, and those components need to work with one another and support each other for the business to succeed. Sometimes, founders start a business because they are good at one or two business components. For example, an individual may be an excellent designer, so they focus on creating excellent websites for clients, or a founder may be a superb cook, so they decide to launch a meal delivery service that specializes in creative, unique, and intriguing dishes. However, if these individuals ignore all other aspects of their businesses, they will fail. A business needs to be understood and managed as a whole with many different yet integrated components. Doing this can be tough, but it can't be ignored.

One way of breaking down and clearly understanding the different components of a new venture is to conceptualize the venture's business model and ensure that the components of that business model not only fit together but also reinforce one another so that each component is more effective when it operates alongside the others.

A business model describes the rationale underlying how an organization creates, delivers, and captures value (Osterwalder and Pigneur, 2010). To make the business model concept clearer and more concrete, Osterwalder and Pigneur (2010) described it as a canvas with nine different building blocks. That canvas is a template for documenting a firm's business model and visualizing how the different elements of the business align to create and capture value. It is a visual chart with elements describing a firm's value proposition, infrastructure, customers, and finances. The different elements of the business model canvas are reflected in Table 12.1.

To make progress as an entrepreneur, it is important to first understand each of these elements for the business you are building and then to configure them in such a way that they support and reinforce one another. To do this, it can be very useful to map out each of these business model elements on the business model canvas, as depicted in Figure 12.1.

Working with this canvas by first specifying and conceptualizing what you will do for each element within the canvas and then developing those elements so they are operational within a venture is how a disparate set of ideas comes together into a substantiable business model. By systematically and deliberately engaging in this process, you can make real progress as an entrepreneur.

The Integration Principle:
Entrepreneurial progress entails *integrating different elements of an idea into a business model.*

The Practice and the Tool

The process of developing an integrated business model for a new venture and using the business model canvas starts with specifying and describing your firm's value proposition and linking that with the clearly identified customer segments you want to serve. The goal here is to try to ensure there is a strong fit between the customers you are targeting and your business's value proposition. Thereafter, it makes sense to identify and describe the channels and customer relationships you can use to reach and work with customers. It is important to ensure those mechanisms work well for the targeted customer segments and hopefully support and enhance the value proposition. Consider whether there are other channels that might

Table 12.1 Components of the Business Model Canvas

Business Model Element	Description
Value Proposition	The collection of products and services a business offers to meet the needs of its customers. A firm's value proposition is what distinguishes it from its competitors. The value proposition provides value through various elements, such as newness, performance, customization, "getting the job done," design, brand, status, price, cost reduction, risk reduction, accessibility, convenience, usability, etc.
Customer Segments	Identification of the customers a firm intends to serve. Various sets of customers can be segmented based on their different needs and attributes. Such segmentation helps ensure appropriate implementation of strategies that meet the characteristics of each selected group of clients. The following are some of the different types of generic customer segments: • *Mass market*: Broad target market, no narrow customer segment targeted. • *Niche market*: Customer segmentation is determined based on the specialized needs and characteristics of clients. • *Segmented*: Additional segmentation is applied within existing customer segments. A business may further distinguish between clients within each segment based on gender, age, income, etc. • *Diverse*: Multiple customer segments with different needs and characteristics are served. • *Multisided platform*: Two mutually dependent customer segments are served by creating a platform to connect them in a way that they provide value to one another (e.g., a credit card company will provide services to credit card holders while also assisting merchants who accept those credit cards).
Channels	The mechanisms a firm uses to get its products or services to customers. Effective channels distribute a company's value proposition in fast, efficient, and cost-effective ways. An organization can reach its customers through either its own channels (storefront), partner channels (major distributors), or a combination of both.

(*continued*)

Table 12.1 Continued

Business Model Element	Description
Customer Relationships	The types of relationship a firm wants to create with its customer segments. The following are different forms of customer relationships: • *Personal assistance*: Assistance is provided in the form of employee-customer interaction. Such assistance is performed either during sales, after sales, or both. • *Self-service*: The relationship is translated from the indirect interaction between the company and its clients. The organization provides the tools its customers need to serve themselves easily and effectively. • *Automated service*: A system similar to self-service is applied but with more personalization as it has the ability to identify individual customers and their preferences. An example is Amazon.com making book suggestions based on the characteristics of the previous book a user purchased. • *Community platform*: The creation of a community allows for direct interaction among different customers and the firm. The community platform allows knowledge to be shared and problems to be solved between different customers. • *Cocreation*: A personal relationship is created through customers' direct input in the final outcomes of the company's products/services.
Key Resources	Key resources are the assets needed to create value for customers. These are things a firm needs to own, lease, license, or hire to be able to create and deliver its value proposition. These resources could be human, financial, physical, and intellectual.
Key Activities	The most important activities a firm must engage in to create and deliver its value proposition. These activities account for the things the firm must *do* to provide its value proposition.
Key Partners	Key partners stem from the relationships a firm fosters to be able to create and deliver its value proposition. Partnerships allow the firm to optimize operations, reduce risks, and focus on its core activities. Key partners may include suppliers, alliance partners, joint venture partners, and other firms or individuals a firm depends on to create and deliver its value proposition.

Table 12.1 Continued

Business Model Element	Description
Revenue Streams	The way a firm makes income from each customer segment. Revenue streams may include the following: • *Asset sale*: Revenue generated from selling ownership rights to a physical good • *Usage fees*: Revenue generated from allowing the use of a particular service • *Subscription fees*: Revenue generated by selling a continuous service • *Lending/leasing/renting*: Revenue generated from giving exclusive rights to an asset for a particular period of time • *Licensing*: Revenue generated from charging for the use of protected intellectual property • *Brokerage fees*: Revenue generated from an intermediate service between two parties • *Advertising*: Revenue generated from charging fees for product advertising
Cost Structure	The costs incurred to deliver, own, and manage the activities, resources, and partnerships needed to provide a firm's value proposition. Costs may be classified as follows: • *Fixed costs*: Costs are unchanged across different applications. • *Variable costs*: Costs vary depending on the amount of production of goods or services. Costs may also be influenced by the following: • *Economies of scale*: Costs go down as the amount of goods ordered or produced increases. • *Economies of scope*: Costs go down due to incorporating other businesses, products, or services related to the original product.

be even more appealing for your target customers or might further enhance the value proposition. From this, specify the different revenue streams you intend to utilize to generate income from the focal customer segments. Are these the most sensible revenue streams? Are there other revenue streams you might be overlooking? After

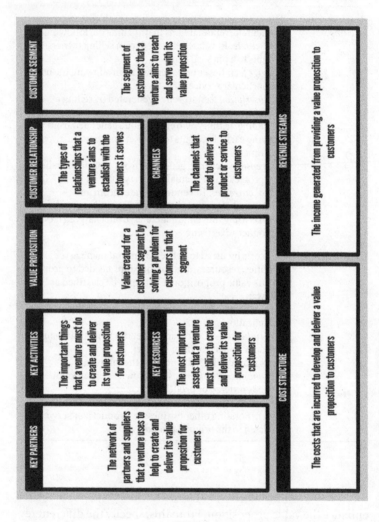

Figure 12.1 The business model canvas.

doing this, you will have the customer-focused components of your business model established.

Next, you need to build out the operational backend aspects of your business model. To do so, identify and describe the key resources, key activities, and key partnerships required to create and deliver the value proposition. Key resources are the assets you need to have access to, key activities are the things you need to do, and key partnerships can fill in for resources and activities that are not under your control. Make sure the resources, activities, and partnerships work well together. Do they support and enhance each other? Finally, identify and describe the different costs incurred to provide the resources, activities, and partnerships to create and deliver the value proposition.

Capture your ideas on a blank version of the business model canvas (e.g., the one in Figure 12.2) and experiment with different ideas for each component until you think you have a viable,

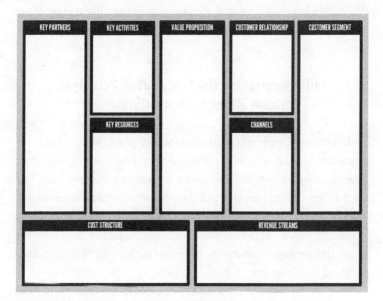

Figure 12.2 Blank version of the business model canvas.

sustainable, and self-reinforcing business model. This can take some time. Few entrepreneurs get their business models right without some experimentation, adaptation, and learning along the way. The goal is to use the business model canvas as a living conceptualization of the business system you are creating and to try to get the system working as effectively and synergistically as possible.

The business model canvas is partly a strategy formulation tool (developing the value proposition and aligning it with customer segments) and partly a strategy execution tool (assessing what channels, relationships, activities, and resources are needed to deliver the value proposition). This interaction between strategy formulation and execution makes for a useful, insightful, and meaningful strategic discussion.

The value of the business model canvas comes from collecting and visualizing all aspects of a business in a single diagram. It forces entrepreneurs to think about all of these aspects together as an integrated system. Further, it creates a platform for founders to debate and clarify how components of a business fit together and whether each component makes sense alongside the other components.

Fully Embracing the Integration Principle on Your Entrepreneurial Journey

To fully embrace the integration principle as you pursue your entrepreneurial endeavor necessitates that you see your new venture as an integrated system with many interacting components. You need to specify and create each aspect of that system such that it works cohesively with the other aspects of the system. The goal is to make the elements of the system stronger together than they are apart. In this way, the different elements of the system should support and reinforce one another.

Fully embracing the integration principle in the entrepreneurial journey entails the following:

- Investing the time and energy to consider and develop each aspect of your business
- Using the business model canvas to create a visual conception of your venture's overall business model
- Experimenting with the different business model elements to develop each element so it works well with the other elements

Ignoring or overlooking the integration principle in the entrepreneurial journey entails the following:

- Only focusing on the aspects of your business that you are good at and ignoring or overlooking other aspects of the business
- Developing different aspects of your business in a haphazard way without considering how they will interact with other aspects of the business
- Never experimenting with different business model components and not being willing to change a business model component when it is not working

Seeing your venture as an integrated system in which the different components not only need to work together but also can actually enhance one another is key to creating a venture that has a competitive advantage over other businesses. It is often easy for a competitor to copy one or two elements of what you do in your business, but it is extremely difficult for another entrepreneur or business to imitate everything you do. Your real advantage will be in the system you create and how the different elements of that system support, reinforce, and enhance one another. That is very difficult for anyone else to emulate.

Conclusion

Can entrepreneurship be distilled down to a core set of ideas or principles that, if applied consistently, would help anyone navigate the complexity and uncertainty of embarking on the entrepreneurial journey? This is the question I set out to answer here. It is a question that has bothered me for the past 20 years through my time initially as a venture founder and then, more recently, as an entrepreneurship educator and researcher. Almost everything I have seen in the entrepreneurship domain to this point has seemed to make entrepreneurship more complex, more nuanced, more sophisticated, and—ultimately—more difficult to understand. I wanted to go the other way—to cut through the noise and the jargon, to get to the core, and to uncover and share simple fundamentals that could help any entrepreneur make meaningful progress in the entrepreneurial journey.

I have spent thousands of hours engaged in and studying entrepreneurial endeavors, and the 12 principles I have shared here are what I view as the core to making progress as a venture founder.

These 12 principles are each quite simple and logical. When explained and shared individually, each most likely makes perfect sense and is not that hard to apply. But in the heat of starting a new venture, when confronted with the triple threat of uncertainty, ambiguity, and resource constraints, it is very easy for any founder to overlook or misapply these principles. This invariably has dire consequences, and it is why so many new ventures fail.

Applying these principles does not guarantee success, but doing so will certainly give you a better chance of making meaningful progress toward a more successful outcome. The principles are not

The Principles of Entrepreneurial Progress. Greg Fisher, Oxford University Press.
© Oxford University Press 2024. DOI: 10.1093/oso/9780197669815.003.0014

magic, and none of them is a silver bullet. They are a means to do things that move a new venture in a productive direction toward sustainability and impact. Ignoring them is a little like ignoring the laws of physics—you might get away with it for a short while, but the oversight will eventually catch up with you. Applying them consistently, however, is an investment in your business, providing a foundation for your venture to create something of real value in a sustainable way. More than that, these principles enhance and reinforce one another—they are synergistic. Applying one of these principles alongside the others makes that principle more effective and more impactful in moving your venture forward. A simple metaphor for this is an attempt to lose weight. To do so, you could embark on an eating plan, exercise more, or increase the amount of water you drink, but the weight loss will be most effective if you do all three. Dieting, exercise, and hydration are most effective for weight loss in the presence of one another. When starting a business, applying the problem principle is most effective when coupled with the exploration, simplicity, and iteration principles, etc. Each of these principles does something to reinforce and enhance the other principles, so to make real progress in moving your venture forward, you should seek to apply and embrace as many of the principles as possible. Trying to apply the principles in isolation without paying attention to the other principles will have a much lesser effect on your entrepreneurial progress than a more holistic application of the principles.

It is also important to recognize that not all the principles are going to be fully relevant all the time. Some principles will be highly relevant in some contexts and only operate in the background in other contexts, and the role of an entrepreneur is to discern when each principle needs to be emphasized. For example, when starting out, the problem principle will be highly salient, but after a core problem is identified and understood, then the problem principle will operate in the background as the other principles are emphasized in the venture development process. Similarly, as one starts building the first iteration of a product offering, the prototype principle becomes highly salient, but once the product is somewhat developed, the prototype principle becomes less salient and other principles take center stage in the venture development process. To properly discern when each principle needs to be emphasized, it is critically important to not only fully understand each of the principles of entrepreneurial progress but also stay alert to what is happening internally and externally in the venture development process.

The Progress Path

A few years back, after spending some time developing, distilling, and understanding the ideas shared in this book, I had an MBA student named Blake come visit me. He had a somewhat similar backstory to Richard, whom I mentioned at the very start of this book. Blake had started his MBA program with the inkling that he ultimately wanted to pursue an entrepreneurial path—to launch a new venture. While pursuing his MBA, he had identified what he thought was a gap in the market for an allergen-free snack or energy bar. The snack and energy bar market had exploded, with many competitors offering similar products, but almost all the options on the market were riddled with nuts and other allergens. Blake himself was extremely allergic to nuts; he had to carry an EpiPen with him all the time, and he couldn't even risk eating something made in a facility with nuts. His snack options were severely limited. Could this be the basis for a new business? he wondered.

This time, instead of fumbling around for wisdom to share or things to say, I prompted Blake to consider and apply many of the principles shared in this book. We spent time talking about and more clearly specifying the problem to be solved: we discussed who has this problem, when they have it, where they are when they need it to be solved, and what they are currently doing to overcome the problem. He defined the problem as a lack of snack options for the 15 million people who suffer from severe food allergies. This is most acute when people are on the go, traveling, commuting, and rushing from one thing to next. It is experienced when people leave the house and in airports, gas stations, and convenience stores. I prompted him to explore and consider multiple different solutions, including trail mix options, cookies, various types of bars, and even solutions more atypical than those.

Although Blake got excited about many of these options and began to envisage a broad product portfolio, he decided to keep things very simple and initially focused on a single product—an energy bar with just three different flavors. Understanding how to create a good-tasting, allergen-free energy bar is not easy. However, the best way to learn is through action, so Blake purchased a blender and a bunch of ingredients and began making bars in his apartment kitchen. These prototype bars weren't just for him. He brought samples to campus and did blind tasting sessions with willing students as participants. From this, he learned about flavor profiles, texture, and other small nuances that matter when creating a bar. Each round of taste testing sent him back to his kitchen to iterate on his recipes.

As he got closer to having a simple bar that tasted good, he began researching manufacturing options during the summer between years one and two of his MBA. Blake also had a consulting internship during this time, which entailed weekly travel, but instead of flying home at the end of each week, he used the opportunity to fly to possible manufacturing facilities. Through this travel, he was able to uncover and make a connection with one of the very few nut-free manufacturing facilities in North America, on the outskirts of Montreal. However, to do a manufacturing run, the facility needed a minimum order size, which necessitated an upfront cash payment.

At the time, Blake did not have the cash on hand, and he also did not know whether he would be able to sell all the bars in the sizable first order. To solve this challenge, he focused on what he did have under his control. He had time, energy, and creativity, plus a large network of friends, classmates, and supporters. To leverage these resources, he decided to launch a crowdfunding campaign on Kickstarter to not only raise the cash needed for the first order from the manufacturer but also test how the idea would be received by others. Therefore, he invested some of his personal savings as well as his time, energy, and creativity into developing a crowdfunding campaign with a powerful personal story, a quirky video, an explanation of the business, and a clear description of the product.

The story touched people, and the campaign, which ran for 30 days, generated more than $40,000. This was enough to cover the first manufacturing run, and it allowed Blake to invest in other aspects of the business. It also gave him some market validation, which he could use when pitching his idea to angel investors. Blake was clear that he wanted this to be a growth business—he wanted to invest in the business and create a brand that would scale. It was for this reason that he sought angel investment funding to allow him to create a platform for growth. If he was trying to create a lifestyle business, he probably would have bootstrapped the business using only his own funds and internally generated resources to establish and grow the business. However, he wanted to create a brand that would grow, expand, and have a national and international reputation and impact. This insight helped him make smart business building and funding decisions.

Throughout this endeavor, Blake had a clear perspective on his business model. He learned about the business model canvas in one of his classes, and he used it to conceptualize and integrate different elements of the business. Each time he decided to change some element of the business model, such as altering the primary channel to market or entering a key partnership, he examined the impact of that change on the rest of the business model. He maintained an integrated perspective.

All these things helped Blake continue to make progress. The progress he made was not smooth and easy. There were many setbacks and difficulties. The business's growth does not represent a smooth hockey stick; it looks more like a messy scribble representing the real startup path referenced in the introduction. However, the end of the scribble—where the business is now—is much higher than where the business started a few years back. The business—Blake's Seed Based—continues to operate, to grow, and to make progress. Blake now has a small but strong team working on the brand. They run a lean operation with many key aspects of the business outsourced to partners. They have contracts to sell their products through many major retailers, and they run a slick, efficient online sales operation. Blake's is now a multi-million-dollar business, but because he is on a growth trajectory, Blake is nowhere near done. He continues to make microbursts of progress from one week to the next such that Blake's Seed Based might continue to grow well into the future.

I strongly believe that all this would not have come to fruition if Blake had not diligently applied the principles laid out in this book. He did not necessarily apply these principles because that is what I or others told him to do; he applied them because they make sense. They are logical. They are fundamental. And applying them diligently pays off. It's not easy, but it reaps benefits.

So, if you wish to embark on an entrepreneurial path, then these principles can help you make progress. They are not silver bullets or secret recipes. They are merely simple, fundamental ideas that enable microbursts of progress on the messy, often challenging path of launching, building, and growing a new venture.

References

Adams, Gabrielle S., Benjamin A. Converse, Andrew H. Hales, and Leidy E. Klotz. 2021. "People Systematically Overlook Subtractive Changes." *Nature* 592 (7853): 258–261.

Albert-Deitch, Cameron. 2019. "This Atlanta Founder's Secret Weapon in Building His $30 Million Company: Growing Up in Nigeria." *Inc Magazine.* https://www.inc.com/magazine/201908/cameron-albert-deitch/tope-awotona-calendly-onl ine-scheduling-venture-capital-nigeria-immigrant.html.

Athletic Brewing. n.d. Accessed October 18, 2021. https://athleticbrewing.com/.

Awotona, Tope. 2020. "Calendly: Tope Awotona." September 11, 2020. *In How I Built This with Guy Raz.* Podcast, MP3 audio. https://www.npr.org/2020/09/11/911960189/calendly-tope-awotona.

Azevedo, Mary Anne. 2021. "Divvy Homes Secures $110M Series C to Help Renters Become Homeowners." TechCrunch. https://techcrunch.com/2021/02/02/divvy-homes-secures-110m-series-c-to-help-renters-become-homeowners/.

Bafera, Julian, and Simon Kleinert. 2023. "Signaling Theory in Entrepreneurship Research: A Systematic Review and Research Agenda." *Entrepreneurship Theory and Practice* 47 (6): 2419–2464.

Bhide, Amar. 2000. *The Origin and Evolution of New Businesses.* New York, NY: Oxford University Press.

Blakely, Sarah. 2017. "Spanx: Sara Blakely." July 3, 2017. In *How I Built This with Guy Raz.* Podcast, MP3 audio. https://www.npr.org/2017/08/15/534771839/spanx-sara-blakely.

Blank, Steve, and Bob Dorf. 2020. *The Startup Owner's Manual: The Step-by-Step Guide for Building a Great Company.* Hoboken, NJ: John Wiley & Sons.

Brown, Tim, and Joey Zwillinger. 2019. "Allbirds: Tim Brown & Joey Zwillinger." June 10, 2019. In *How I Built This with Guy Raz.* Podcast, MP3 audio. https://www.npr.org/2019/06/07/730695224/allbirds-tim-brown-joey-zwillinger.

Burnell, Devin, Emily Neubert, and Greg Fisher. 2023. "Venture Tales: Practical Storytelling Strategies Underpinning Entrepreneurial Narratives." *Business Horizons* 66 (3): 325–346.

Burnell, Devin, Regan Stevenson, and Greg Fisher. 2023. "Early-Stage Business Model Experimentation and Pivoting." *Journal of Business Venturing* 38 (4): 106314.

Burns, Luke. 2017. "Additions to the Journalistic 5W's." *New Yorker,* January 31, 2017. Accessed September 18, 2021. https://www.newyorker.com/humor/daily-shouts/additions-to-the-five-journalistic-ws.

Butterfield, Stewart. 2017. "The Big Pivot—Slack's Stewart Butterfield." In *Masters of Scale with Reed Hoffman.* Podcast. https://mastersofscale.com/stewart-butt erfield-the-big-pivot/.

Canva Website. n.d. Accessed June 2022. https://www.canva.com/about/.

CB Insights. 2021. "The Top 12 Reasons Startups Fail." Accessed September 18, 2021. https://www.cbinsights.com/reports/CB-Insights_Top-Reasons-Start ups-Fail.pdf.

Chalkin, Max. 2013. "True to Its Roots: Why Kickstarter Won't Sell." Fast Company. Accessed August 21, 2021. https://www.fastcompany.com/3006694/true-to-its-roots-why-kickstarter-wont-sell.

Chandler, Gaylen N., Dawn R. DeTienne, Alexander McKelvie, and Troy V. Mumford. 2011. "Causation and Effectuation Processes: A Validation Study." *Journal of Business Venturing* 26 (3): 375–390.

Clarke, Jean. 2011. "Revitalizing Entrepreneurship: How Visual Symbols Are Used in Entrepreneurial Performances." *Journal of Management Studies* 48 (6): 1365–1391.

Clear, James. "First Principles: Elon Musk on the Power of Thinking for Yourself." Accessed December 30, 2023. https://jamesclear.com/first-principles.

CNBC. 2021. "How I Sold My Start-Up to Lululemon for $500 Million." April 19, 2021. Accessed August 12, 2021. https://www.youtube.com/watch?v=HgWo LqZILk8.

Cope, Jason. 2005. "Toward a Dynamic Learning Perspective of Entrepreneurship." *Entrepreneurship Theory and Practice* 29 (4): 373–397.

CritBuns. n.d. "About Critbuns." Accessed September 12, 2021. http://www.critb uns.com/about.html.

Eisenhardt, Kathleen M., and Rory M. McDonald. 2020. "The New-Market Conundrum." *Harvard Business Review* 98 (3): 75–83.

Erikson, Gary. 2018. "Clif Bar: Gary Erickson." In *How I Built This with Guy Raz*. Podcast, MP3 audio. https://www.npr.org/2018/02/06/572560919/clif-bar-gary-erickson.

Farnam Street. n.d. "Complexity Bias: Why We Prefer Complicated to Simple." *Farnam Street* (blog). Accessed August 12, 2021. https://fs.blog/complexity-bias/.

Farnam Street. n.d. "Elon Musk on How to Build Knowledge." *Farnam Street* (blog). Accessed August 11, 2021. https://fs.blog/2015/01/elon-musk-knowledge/.

Farnam Street. n.d. "How to Use Occam's Razor Without Getting Cut." *Farnam Street* (blog). Accessed August 14, 2021. https://fs.blog/occams-razor/.

Fiol, C. Marlene. 2002. "Capitalizing on Paradox: The Role of Language in Transforming Organizational Identities." *Organization Science* 13 (6): 653–666.

Fisher, Greg. 2012. "Effectuation, Causation, and Bricolage: A Behavioral Comparison of Emerging Theories in Entrepreneurship Research." *Entrepreneurship Theory and Practice* 36 (5): 1019–1051.

Fisher, Greg, and Michael Goldman. 2013. *Beyond Epic: Building the Business Beyond a Single Event* (Case Study). London, Ontario: Ivey Publishing.

Fisher, Greg, Emily Neubert, and Devin Burnell. 2021. "Resourcefulness Narratives: Transforming Actions into Stories to Mobilize Support." *Journal of Business Venturing* 36 (4): 106122.

Fisher, Greg, Regan Stevenson, and Devin Burnell. 2020. "Permission to Hustle: Igniting Entrepreneurship in an Organization." *Journal of Business Venturing Insights* 14: e00173.

Fisher, Greg, Regan Stevenson, Emily Neubert, Devin Burnell, and Donald F. Kuratko. 2020. "Entrepreneurial Hustle: Navigating Uncertainty and Enrolling Venture Stakeholders through Urgent and Unorthodox Action." *Journal of Management Studies* 57 (5): 1002–1036.

Fixson, Sebastian K., and Tucker J. Marion. 2016. "A Case Study of Crowdsourcing Gone Wrong." *Harvard Business Review Digital Articles*, 2–5.

Fooddive Website. 2021. "Nonalcoholic Beer Maker Athletic Brewing Raises $50M." Accessed October 18, 2021. https://www.fooddive.com/news/nonalcoholic-beer-maker-athletic-brewing-raises-50m/601050/.

Garber, Megan. 2014. "Instagram Was First Called 'Burbn.'" *The Atlantic*. Accessed April 25, 2021. https://www.theatlantic.com/technology/archive/2014/07/instagram-used-to-be-called-brbn/373815/.

Garud, Raghu, and Antonio Paco Giuliani. 2013. "A Narrative Perspective on Entrepreneurial Opportunities." *Academy of Management Review* 38 (1): 157–160.

Garud, Raghu, Henri A. Schildt, and Theresa K. Lant. 2014. "Entrepreneurial Storytelling, Future Expectations, and the Paradox of Legitimacy." *Organization Science* 25 (5): 1479–1492.

Gebbia, Joe. 2016. "How Airbnb Designs for Trust." Filmed February 2016 in Vancouver, BC. TED Video, 2:49. https://www.ted.com/talks/joe_gebbia_how_airbnb_designs_for_trust.

Gebbia, Joe. 2017. "Airbnb: Joe Gebbia." August 28, 2017. In *How I Built This with Guy Raz*. Podcast, MP3 audio, 3:31. https://www.npr.org/2017/10/19/543035808/airbnb-joe-gebbia.

Gilbert, Clark G., and Matthew J. Eyring. 2010. "Beating the Odds When You Launch a New Venture." *Harvard Business Review* 88 (5): 93–98.

Gilboa, David, and David Blumenthal. 2018. Warby Parker: Dave Gilboa & Neil Blumenthal. *How I Built This Podcast with Guy Raz*. National Public Radio. https://www.npr.org/2018/03/26/586048422/warby-parker-dave-gilboa-neil-blumenthal.

Graham, Paul. 2008. "Six Principles for Making New Things." February 2008. Accessed May 12, 2021. http://www.paulgraham.com/newthings.html?viewfullsite=1.

Grant, Adam. 2016. "Six Secrets to True Originality." People and Organizational Performance. McKinsey & Company. August 5, 2016. Accessed August 14, 2021. https://www.mckinsey.com/business-functions/people-and-organizational-performance/our-insights/six-secrets-to-true-originality.

Grimes, Matthew G. October 2018. "The Pivot: How Founders Respond to Feedback through Idea and Identity Work." *Academy of Management Journal* 61 (5): 1692–1717.

The Guardian. 2016. "YouTube Was Meant to Be a Video-Dating Website." March 2016. Accessed March 10, 2022. https://www.theguardian.com/technology/2016/mar/16/youtube-past-video-dating-website.

Hall, Kindra. 2019. *Stories That Stick: How Storytelling Can Captivate Customers, Influence Audiences, and Transform Your Business*. Nashville, TN: HarperCollins Leadership.

Handley, Lucy. 2020. "Dave Gilboa and Neil Blumenthal: A Vision for Business." CNBC. https://www.cnbc.com/warby-parkers-dave-gilboa-and-neil-blument hal-a-vision-for-business/.

Hart, Myra, Michael J. Roberts, and Julia D. Stevens. 2003. *Zipcar: Refining the Business Model.* Cambridge, MA: Harvard Business School.

Heath, Chip, and Dan Heath. 2013. *Decisive: How to Make Better Choices in Life and Work.* New York: Random House.

Hefets, Adena 2021. "Divvy Homes CEO & Co-Founder: Adena Hefets." In *ExecuTalks*. Podcast. https://www.executalks.com/episodes/adena-hefets.

Huddleston, Tom Jr. 2018. "How Allbirds Went from Silicon Valley Fashion Staple to a $1.4 Billion Sneaker Start-up." The Upstarts. December 18, 2018. Accessed April 6, 2021. https://www.cnbc.com/2018/12/14/allbirds-went-from-silicon-valley-staple-to-billion-sneaker-startup.html.

Khan, Omer. 2019. "Calendly's Founder: Building a $30M SaaS after 3 Failed Startups." https://saasclub.io/podcast/calendlys-founder-finding-saas-success-after-failed-startups/.

Kickstarter. "Kickstarter FAQ—The Basics." Internet Archive Wayback Machine. Accessed August 21, 2021. https://web.archive.org/web/20090925174723/http://www.kickstarter.com/learn-more.

Kickstarter. "Stats." Accessed September 15, 2021. https://www.kickstarter.com/help/stats.

Kirtley, Jacqueline, and Siobhan O'Mahony. 2023. "What Is a Pivot? Explaining When and How Entrepreneurial Firms Decide to Make Strategic Change and Pivot." *Strategic Management Journal* 44 (1): 197–230.

Kirzner, Israel M. 1999. "Creativity and/or Alertness: A Reconsideration of the Schumpeterian Entrepreneur." *Review of Austrian Economics* 11 (1–2): 5–17.

Klotz, Leidy. 2021. *Subtract: The Untapped Science of Less.* New York: Flatiron Books.

Knapp, Jake, John Zeratsky, and Braden Kowitz. 2016. *Sprint: How to Solve Big Problems and Test New Ideas in Just Five Days.* New York: Simon and Schuster.

Lafley, Alan G., Roger L. Martin, Jan W. Rivkin, and Nicolaj Siggelkow. 2012. "Bringing Science to the Art of Strategy." *Harvard Business Review* 90 (9): 56–66.

Latimore, Marshall A. 2021. "Atlanta-Based Calendly Valued at $3 Billion Following $350-Million Round of Investment." *Atlanta Voice.* https://www.thea tlantavoice.com/articles/atlanta-based-calendly-valued-at-3-billion-following-350-million-round-of-investment/.

Liedtka, Jeanne, and Tim Ogilvie. 2011. *Designing for Growth: A Design Thinking Tool Kit for Managers.* New York: Columbia University Press.

Lincoln, Sadie. 2018. Barre3: Sadie Lincoln. In *How I Built This with Guy Raz.* Podcast, MP3 audio. https://www.npr.org/2018/11/01/663028736/barre3-sadie-lincoln.

Lockwood, Christi, and Jean-François Soublière, eds. 2022. *Advances in Cultural Entrepreneurship.* Northampton, MA: Emerald Publishing Limited.

Lohr, Steve. 2015. "Quirky, an Invention Startup, Files for Bankruptcy." *New York Times.* September 23, 2015. Accessed May 2, 2021. https://www.nytimes.com/2015/09/23/business/the-invention-start-up-quirky-files-for-bankruptcy.html.

Lounsbury, Michael, and Mary Ann Glynn. 2001. "Cultural Entrepreneurship: Stories, Legitimacy, and the Acquisition of Resources." *Strategic Management Journal* 22 (6–7): 545–564.

Lunden, Ingrid. 2021. "How Atlanta's Calendly Turned a Scheduling Nightmare into a $3B Startup." TechCrunch. https://techcrunch.com/2021/01/26/how-atlantas-calendly-turned-a-scheduling-nightmare-into-a-3b-startup/.

Magnus, Steve. Accessed September 12, 2021. https://twitter.com/stevemagness/status/1437028120956182528.

Mantere, Saku, Pekka Aula, Henri Schildt, and Eero Vaara. 2013. "Narrative Attributions of Entrepreneurial Failure." *Journal of Business Venturing* 28 (4): 459–473.

McDonald, Rory M., and Kathleen M. Eisenhardt. 2020. "Parallel Play: Startups, Nascent Markets, and Effective Business-Model Design." *Administrative Science Quarterly* 65 (2): 483–523.

McDonald, Rory, and Cheng Gao. 2019. "Pivoting Isn't Enough? Managing Strategic Reorientation in New Ventures." *Organization Science* 30 (6): 1289–1318.

McKeown, Greg. 2021. *Effortless: Make It Easier to Do What Matters Most.* New York: Currency.

Mills, Adam J., and Joby John. 2020. "Brand Stories: Bringing Narrative Theory to Brand Management." *Journal of Strategic Marketing*, 1–19. https://doi.org/10.1080/0965254X.2020.1853201.

Mills, Adam J., and Joby John. 2023. "Revisiting Brand Origin: Expanding the Strategic Portfolio of Brand-Level Attributes." *Journal of Strategic Marketing* 31 (6): 1220–1237.

Morris, Michael H., and Donald F. Kuratko. 2020. *What Do Entrepreneurs Create?: Understanding Four Types of Ventures.* Northampton, MA: Edward Elgar Publishing.

Mullin, Benjamin, Joe Flint, and Maureen Farrell. 2020. "Quibi Is Shutting Down Barely Six Months after Going Live." *Wall Street Journal.* October 22, 2020. Accessed September 20, 2021. https://www.wsj.com/articles/quibi-weighs-shutting-down-as-problems-mount-11603301946.

Murrell, Jerry. 2019. "Five Guys: Jerry Murrell." In *How I Built This* with Guy Raz. Podcast. https://www.npr.org/2019/01/11/684560464/five-guys-jerry-murrell.

Navis, Chad, and Mary Ann Glynn. 2011. "Legitimate Distinctiveness and the Entrepreneurial Identity: Influence on Investor Judgments of New Venture Plausibility." *Academy of Management Review* 36 (3): 479–499.

Nguyen, Ally. 2020. "Adena Hefets in Action to Change How Americans Look at Homeownership." EnvZone. https://envzone.com/adena-hefets-in-action-to-change-how-americans-look-at-homeownership/.

Nightline. 1999. "IDEO: Shopping Cart Design Process." YouTube. Accessed September 11, 2021. https://www.youtube.com/watch?v=izjhx17NuSE.

Osterwalder, Alexander, and Yves Pigneur. 2010. *Business Model Generation: A Handbook for Visionaries, Game Changers, and Challengers.* Vol. 1. Hoboken, NJ: John Wiley & Sons.

Parrish, Shane. 2019. *The Great Mental Models Volume 1: General Thinking Concepts.* Ontario, CA: Lattice Work Publishing.

Perkins, Melanie. 2021. "Canva: Melanie Perkins." March 1, 2021. In *How I Built This with Guy Raz*. Podcast, MP3 audio. https://www.npr.org/2021/02/26/971813519/canva-melanie-perkins-2019.

Putnam, Brynn. 2020. "Brynn Putnam, CEO of Mirror, on Launching a Breakout Growth Smart Hardware Device for Fitness." In *Breakthrough Growth*. Podcast. Accessed May 17, 2021. https://breakoutgrowth.castos.com/episodes/brynn-putnam-ceo-of-mirror-on-launching-a-breakout-growth-smart-hardware-dev ice-for-fitness.

Ries, Eric. 2011. *The Lean Startup: How Today's Entrepreneurs Use Continuous Innovation to Create Radically Successful Businesses*. New York: Currency.

Rubio, Jen. 2019. "Away: Jen Rubio." March 8, 2019. In *How I Built This with Guy Raz*. Podcast, MP3 audio. https://www.npr.org/2019/03/08/701651787/away-jen-rubio.

Ruffner, Zoe. 2018. "Now, There's a Mirror That Beams Live Fitness Classes into Your Home." October 15, 2018. Accessed May 24, 2021. https://www.vogue.com/article/mirror-fitness-at-home-exercise-work-out.

Salazar, M. (Host). 2020. "Athletic Brewing: Pioneering a Non-Alcoholic Craft Beer Revolution with Bill Shufelt." *For All Drinks* Podcast. https://open.spotify.com/episode/0xP19r80gNjopHbl4qBZuV?si=wrE2KariTIKPU_RWKZWNfg.

Sarasvathy, Saras D. 2001. "Causation and Effectuation: Toward a Theoretical Shift from Economic Inevitability to Entrepreneurial Contingency." *Academy of Management Review* 26 (2): 243–263.

Sarasvathy, Saras D. 2009. *Effectuation: Elements of Entrepreneurial Expertise*. Northampton, MA: Edward Elgar Publishing.

Sarasvathy, Saras D., and Nicholas Dew. 2006. *The Affordable Loss Principle. Technical Note*. Charlottesville, VA: University of Virginia Darden School Foundation.

Sawers, P. 2021. "Calendly's Automated Meeting Scheduler Gets New Enterprise Features." Venture Beat. https://venturebeat.com/2021/05/03/calendlys-automated-meeting-scheduler-gets-new-enterprise-features/.

Scudamore, Brian. 2018. "1-800-GOT-JUNK?: Brian Scudamore." In *How I Built This with Guy Raz*. Podcast, MP3 audio. https://www.npr.org/2018/06/07/590234095/1-800-got-junk-brian-scudamore.

Shepherd, Dean A., Stella K. Seyb, and Gerard George. 2023. "Grounding Business Models: Cognition, Boundary Objects, and Business Model Change." *Academy of Management Review* 48 (1): 100–122.

Shepherd, Dean A., Trenton Williams, Marcus Wolfe, and Holger Patzelt. 2016. *Learning from Entrepreneurial Failure*. Cambridge, UK: Cambridge University Press.

Shufelt, Bill. 2020. "Bill Shufelt of Athletic Brewing." In *Drink Beer, Think Beer* Podcast with John Holl (Host). Episode 13. https://www.beeredge.com/podcasts/drink-beer-think-beer/.

Silver, David. A. 1985. *Entrepreneurial Megabucks*. New York: Wiley.

SPARK Schools. n.d. "Our Story." Accessed September 18, 2021. https://sparkschools.co.za/our-story/.

Spina, Chiara, Arnaldo Camuffo, and Alfonso Gambardella. 2020. "Founders, Apply the Scientific Method to Your Start-up." *Harvard Business Review Digital Articles*, November 18, 2020, 2–5.

Sridharan, Karthik. Accessed May 22, 2021. https://twitter.com/KarthikS2206/status/1396095567256641536.

Stinchcombe, Arthur L. 1965. "Social Structure and Organizations." In *Handbook of Organizations (RLE: Organizations)*, 142–193. Routledge.

Suchman, Mark C. 1995. "Managing Legitimacy: Strategic and Institutional Approaches." *Academy of Management Review* 20 (3): 571–610.

Systrom, Kevin. "How to Keep It Simple While Scaling Big." In *Masters of Scale*. Podcast, MP3 audio. Accessed June 14, 2021. https://mastersofscale.com/kevin-systrom-how-to-keep-it-simple-while-scaling-big/.

Systrom, Kevin. 2019. "The Tim Ferriss Show Transcripts: Kevin Systrom (#369)." April 30, 2019. In *The Tim Ferris Show*. Podcast, MP3 audio. Accessed March 3, 2021. https://tim.blog/2019/04/30/the-tim-ferriss-show-transcripts-kevin-systrom-369/.

Systrom, Kevin, and Mike Kreiger. 2017. "Instagram: Kevin Systrom & Mike Krieger." November 13, 2017. In *How I Built This with Guy Raz*. Podcast, MP3 audio. https://www.npr.org/2018/01/02/562887933/instagram-kevin-systrom-mike-krieger.

Tamaseb, Ali. 2021. *Super Founders: What Data Reveals about Billion-Dollar Startups*. New York: PublicAffairs.

Zott, Christoph, and Raphael Amit. 2008. "The Fit between Product Market Strategy and Business Model: Implications for Firm Performance." *Strategic Management Journal* 29 (1): 1–26.

Zott, Christoph, and Quy Nguyen Huy. 2007. "How Entrepreneurs Use Symbolic Management to Acquire Resources." *Administrative Science Quarterly* 52 (1): 70–105.

Index